HAUNTED
ROTHERHAM

HAUNTED ROTHERHAM

Richard Bramall & Joe Collins

The History Press

*We would like to dedicate this book to the good people of Rotherham, our long-suffering
wives who have had to put up with all the late nights while we wrote it, plus all the friends
we have dragged along in the freezing cold on our ghosts hunts over the years.*

*Also, our warmest thanks and deepest respect must go to the departed souls
who returned from the dead and kept us up late into the night.*

Without all of your help, there would be no Haunted Rotherham.

First published 2011

The History Press
The Mill, Brimscombe Port
Stroud, Gloucestershire, GL5 2QG
www.thehistorypress.co.uk

© Richard Bramall & Joe Collins, 2011

The right of Richard Bramall & Joe Collins, to be identified
as the Authors of this work has been asserted in accordance with
the Copyrights, Designs and Patents Act 1988.

ISBN 978 0 7524 6117 5
Typesetting and origination by The History Press
Printed in Malta.

Contents

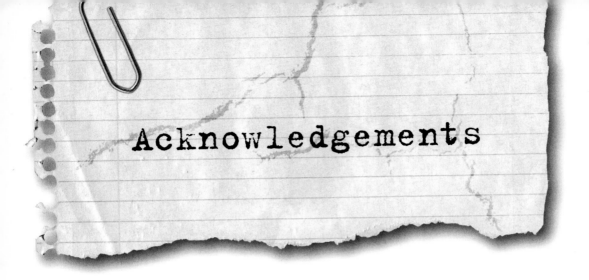

Acknowledgements

WE would like to thank all the visitors to Rotherham-ghosts.com website and its subsidiaries that have supported us over the years and helped us create a good knowledge of hauntings throughout South Yorkshire, there are too many people to mention but not enough thanks can be given.

We would also like to thank the former members of Dearne Valley Paranormal Investigations team and Sheffield Paranormal for their help throughout this crusade.

The following people and organisations have supplied us with a more detailed account of some of the events which make this book more interesting:

Individuals
Paul Collins
Mrs X
Jo Kay

Newspapers
Sheffield Star
Rotherham Star
South Yorkshire Times
Rotherham Advertiser (Mr Melloy, Editor)
Dearne Valley Weekender

Aditional Organisations
The National Trust
Rotherhamweb.co.uk
Rotherham Archives

Plus, all the people who supplied us with information yet wish to remain anonymous.

And finally, thanks to you the reader for purchasing our book, we hope you enjoy reading it as much as we did writing it.

Introduction

THE British Isles are arguably amongst the most haunted parts of the world and Rotherham plays a big part in this – this book is aimed at everyone interested in the spectres and phantoms that inhabit Rotherham's homes, pubs, offices and highways.

When you ask people if they believe in ghosts, you will often be greeted by one of the following replies: 'There's no such thing!', 'There's something but I don't know what', or 'Yes, I have seen one!' The reactions of people who witness ghosts, and especially those who have been involved with demonic cases, are not always quick to reveal their true beliefs because they often feel embarrassment, humiliation or even guilt.

Unfortunately we live in a society that seems to ridicule and dismiss such reports right from the start. Many people, including figures of authority and larger organisations, do not want the public to be privy to such information. Neither do some individuals want their best friends or close relatives to know of their plight, sometimes going to great lengths to cover up stories to prevent the truth. However, we are putting some of these stories in print, though some of the names and locations have been changed to protect identity.

From an early age, Richard Bramall experienced a number of unexplainable apparitions, some terrifying. This was treated as imaginary friends by his family; even though they became less frequent as he grew older, they carried on into his early teens. He started to research reported sightings in the Rotherham area to see if others had had similar encounters. To feed his hunger to prove the existence of life after death, Richard founded the Rotherham-ghosts. com website in January 2004, where he could share information with others, hoping that they would come forward with their reports.

Due to a traumatic paranormal experience as a child, dismissed by his parents and teachers alike, Joe Collins was compelled to provide evidence that what he witnessed during this time was not a 'dream' or his 'imagination'. This fired him into an obsession with the paranormal and lead him to read countless books on the supernatural and search endless websites to track down recorded sightings of ghosts which would provide evidence to support his claim of the incidents that he had witnessed as a child.

We finally met in 2006, when our obsession with the paranormal brought us together through a mutual friend, Gary Crompton, a former college classmate of Joe's, who had being working alongside Richard in a paranormal group.

We soon realised that our paths had crossed many times before. Sharing the same interest in the paranormal, we had unknowingly swapped a large amount of information through third parties and forums and, in turn, had visited and investigated reports published by the other.

We have been working together since 2006 and have collated our information in this book, which we hope you will enjoy.

Richard Bramall and Joe Collins, 2011
www.ROTHERHAM-GHOSTS.com

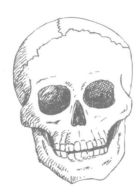

1

Aston

THE village of Aston is situated close to the M1, a few miles south of Rotherham. There has been a church there since about the year AD 700 and in the Domesday survey of 1086 the village, then known as 'Estone', was recorded as being an area of arable pasture and woodland, with a value of eight shillings. Aston was traditionally a farming village and a large number of old farm buildings survive along the main road. Several distinguished and beautiful structures are cared for today as private residences. 'High Trees', on the corner of Church Lane, is a grand old house commonly referred to as 'The White House' by villagers, and has been the subject of many ghost stories among village children for decades. Not too far away from this is Aston Hall, which has many ghost stories attached to it too.

The Bloody Rage of Aston Rectory

The former rectory, now known as 'High Trees', is haunted by the ghost of a rector, who caught his wife in the arms of the butler and murdered her.

The vicar of Aston was an upstanding pillar of the community and was very highly thought of at that time; many people aspired to be like him and envied his privileged lifestyle and family values, not to mention his beautiful wife, whom he doted on.

One Sunday morning his wife told him that she was feeling ill. Concerned, the vicar told his wife to stay in bed that morning and said that he would conduct mass alone. This is something that he rarely did as his wife was always by his side. After attending to his wife, he hurried across to the church, where the parishioners were waiting for their morning service. Just as the service was about to begin, he suddenly realised that he had forgotten his glasses and remembered that they were on the bedside table. He instructed his organist to start the first hymn whilst he slipped away through the side door to rush home and collect his spectacles.

He entered the rectory quietly, not wanting to wake his ill wife, crept up the stairs and headed towards the bedroom door. Much to his surprise, he heard the voice of a man coming from inside the room. A little confused by this, he opened the door and found his wife in the arms of the butler. Angered and upset by the sight, he went into a rage and physically threw the butler down the stairs. Picking himself off the floor, the butler ran out through the front door and was never seen in the village again. The vicar's wife began protesting her innocence, stating that the butler had tried to force himself onto her. But her pleas fell on deaf ears. The vicar was consumed with raged by what he had seen and grabbed a knife off the breakfast tray that was situated at the side of the bed. Fearing for her life, his wife ran for the staircase, but was soon caught by the vicar. He grabbed her by her hair, pulled her head backwards and began slashing her throat. With blood pouring from the wound, he then threw her down the stairs and left her to bleed to death while he returned to carry on with the service.

To this day, the bloodstain remains at the foot of the stairs and cannot be removed by any form of cleaning. The vicar and his wife are said to haunt the property. She haunts the stairway and bedroom, while his spirit is said to walk the perimeter walls and grounds, horrified by what sins they committed.

Local legend says that as long as the bloodstain remains on the floor, the vicar will remain forever and a day for every drop of blood that he spilt.

Aston Hall Hotel

Located on the outskirts of Rotherham, on Worksop Road, adjacent to the church, sits a grand eighteenth-century hall, which was designed by distinguished architect John Carr. Originally, a much older structure had occupied the same position, but was destroyed by fire. The structure of the hall was continually being altered and added to until 1825, and has previously been used as a large country house, hospital, and, most recently, a hotel and restaurant.

Ason rectory as it is today. (Authors' collection)

Photogenic Phantom

Around 1963, this building was put up for sale and a photographer was sent to take pictures of the old building. At the time the hall was locked and most of the furniture and other effects had been removed. The photographer was a professional who did a lot of freelance work for Sheffield newspapers. Upon arriving he set up a large plate camera on the front lawn and took two pictures, before stopping for a moment to admire the grounds and scenery around the historical home. After returning to his studio to develop the prints, he noticed a figure in one of the photographs, staring at the camera from an upstairs window. This confused him as he knew there was no one in the building, not to mention the fact that it was boarded up and he had had to acquire a key just to enter the gardens alone!

He set about enlarging the shot of the window and printed it off again and was flabbergasted at what he saw. What lay before him was the ghost of a man dressed in seventeenth-century clothing! He passed the picture on to the editor of the *Sheffield Star*, who at first refused to publish the story due to the absence of sufficient background information to the report. Some time later, the photographer found an old painted portrait that came from Aston Hall and noticed that the figure corresponded with the one in the photograph. He passed the information on to the editor, who then published the story. This created a lot of media interest and several other local newspapers also ran the story.

The Murder Tunnels

A woman, who once worked at Aston Hall as a lady's maid, knew some of the darker secrets of the hall's past and recounted her tales to a number of older residents who still live in Aston today.

Many years ago the lady of the house, Lady Pagett, is rumoured to have fallen in love with a butler, who then murdered her in an underground tunnel which ran from the old rectory to Aston Hall after she threatened to reveal their affair. Some of the previous residents of Aston Cottage, which is built over the site of the tunnels, claim to have heard the screams of a woman and the sounds of her running footsteps emanating from 'underground' at certain times of the year.

If Lady Pagett was indeed engaged in such an illicit affair, then her family would quite naturally have covered up the scandal by closing ranks and stone-walling any enquiries. No murder charge was ever brought, but strangely she was never seen in the village again.

What is it with Aston and their butlers?

Darkness in the Cellar

Most old halls have a chequered history, but not many can claim they were once a lunatic asylum. Years ago Aston Hall was just this, and many ghost stories surround the hall's cellars and their previous use.

When the hall was being renovated prior to it becoming a hotel, there was a problem with flooding in the cellar and so a builder went down to carry out some works and clear out the channels cut into the stone floor. He was struck by what looked like a stone altar that stood in the centre of the room at the back. Looking at the strange relic, he wondered what this could have been used for.

All of a sudden a dark figure appeared and lent over the slab, as if looking for an offering on the table. He described it as a dark, shadowy shape, around six feet tall with piercing red eyes. Terrified at this encounter, he ran back up the stairs to be greeted by a member of staff. He told her of his ordeal, and she informed him that the hall used to be a mental institution, and that the cellar where he'd been working was once used to perform post-mortems. The stone slab was to 'lay out' the dead and the channels were there to take away the bodily fluids.

Could this have been the ghost of Lady Pecket, who is said to wander the tunnels leading to the cellar, or was it a dark entity waiting to welcome the spirit of a newly deceased person from the asylum?

Lunatic of Ulley Reservoir

During the late-nineteenth century, conditions in asylums were poor. The patients were treated brutally and often experimented on due to the lack of understanding of their medical condition. This usually made their state of mind much worse.

A ghost is alleged to haunt the bridge at Ulley Reservoir. It is said to be that of a psychopath, who escaped from Aston Hall when it was a lunatic asylum in the early 1900s.

The story goes that during routine lights out one night, one of the patients was being moved to a more secure wing after an earlier disturbance, when he broke free from his restraints and made his escape by jumping out of a first-floor window.

Staff, worried for the safety of the public, quickly formed a search party and a manhunt soon ensued. They followed the madman across the scrubland and moor and eventually cornered him with the help of some local farm labourers. Fearing his capture, the man climbed onto the wall of the bridge in a bid to evade his pursuers. Realising that there was no escape, and not wanting to be taken back, he plunged straight into the murky depths of the reservoir. Despite a frantic search by torchlight, they could not find him until his bloated body was washed up days later.

Today, his ghost is said to be seen running around the roads and paths leading on to the bridge, until he gets to the centre, at which point he hurls himself off into the water.

Ulley Reservoir, where the ghost of a mad man is said to throw himself off the bridge. (Authors' collection)

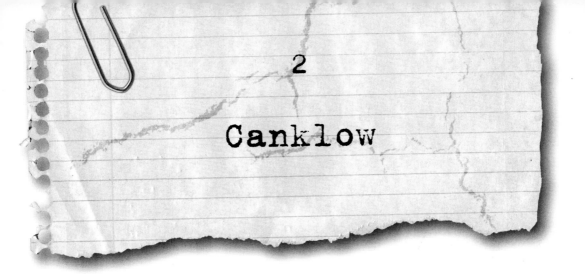

2

Canklow

The Secret Chamber of Haworth Hall

Haworth Hall, seat of the Haworth family for several generations, had a haunted reputation which lives on to this day in the memories of all those who remember it. It was situated in Canklow Meadows, Rotherham for more than 340 years, before its demolition in 1965 to make way for the M1 motorway. It was used as a refugee station during the First World War and then a boarding school prior to it being occupied by the Mountain family.

In Elizabethan times, daughter of the house Elaine Haworth was brutally murdered by her jealous suitor, Sir Herbert Vayne, who was then tried and sent to his death at York city gallows for her murder. Not long after her death, residents of the hall reported heavy footsteps and the rustle of long dresses echoing from the old, dark rooms on the second floor of the hall. This continued for several generations.

At the beginning of the eighteenth century, it is said that Miss Cecilia Kitson, one of the hall's occupants, discovered a secret room behind the large fireplace in the dining room. It was fully furnished, including a large bed on which the curious investigator was horrified to find a skeleton, believed to be that of William Haworth, Catholic priest and brother of the murdered Elaine. He had been in hiding due to his faith at the time of Elaine's murder and the location of the secret room was only known to his sister. His disappearance had therefore been a mystery until his remains were stumbled across by Cecilia many, many years later.

There is a strange echo here of the much better-known story of Minster Lovell Hall, in Oxfordshire, where Francis Lovell is reputed to have fled for safety after the Battle of Stoke, secreting himself in a hidden room whose whereabouts was known only to an aged and trusty servant. The retainer unfortunately died that very night, leaving Lovell to perish of starvation, only being discovered in 1708 when workmen, making alterations, broke unexpectedly into the room, finding a skeleton in rags, seated at a table over an open book, all of which, rags, books, skeleton, and table, faded to dust with the inrush of air, before their very eyes. Rooms of this nature weren't uncommon back then and were known as priest holes. Many were in private houses and some still exist.

Whilst trying to authenticate this story we stumbled across some extracts from the

Rotherham Advertiser that were published on 31 December 1971. These accounts seem to clarify the story's creditability:

Few stories are more fascinating than the legend of Howarth Hall, the lovely, yet tragic house – demolished in 1965 – which for centuries stood in isolation on Canklow Meadows. Details of the legend are contained in an old manuscript which came into the possession of the Mountain family – the last occupants of the haunted hall.

It tells the story of Sir Hubert Vayne of Tickhill Grange, Tickhill, who died on the scaffold at York for the murder of the woman he wanted to marry. Vayne died on the common gallows for the murder of young Elaine Howarth of Howarth Hall, near Rotherham.

The script, a copy of which has been given to the *Advertiser* by Mr Oswald Parkin, of Morthen, reveals the full tragic story of Howarth Hall and a ghost which still walked the floors of the hall, even in the twentieth century.

Although Mrs E.G. Mountain never saw the spectre when she lived at Howarth Hall, she says that her late husband, Mr

Howarth Hall; most of the land was used to build the slip road for the M1 motorway. (Authors' collection)

R.D. Mountain, her daughter, Christine, and visitors claimed to have seen it or heard it. Sceptics may scoff. But Mr Mountain (who used to be in business as a butcher with his father, the late Mr C.D. Mountain, who also lived at the hall) was convinced that it was haunted.

There are stories of mysterious footsteps and of tight fitting doors suddenly rattling. Daughter Christine once felt something go past her. One Christmas, a relative woke in the middle of the night and said afterwards that there was a figure at the bottom of the bed beckoning to her. She never stayed there again.

If the house was haunted, there is little wonder, as readers will see for themselves after reading the legend of Howarth Hall.

The Legend and Tragedy of Howarth Hall

Few local stories are sadder than the history of Father Wilfred Howarth, the Jesuit Priest of Howarth Hall. The reign of Elizabeth was marked by terrible penal laws against the emissaries and the adherents of the Church of Rome. More political and religious prosecutions were carried on by the State. Very often, penal laws were evoked for the purpose of personal spite and revenge, and not to safeguard either personal liberty or religious freedom. An example of this is the tragedy we now tell.

A special feature of interest in Howarth Hall is the oaken wainscot of the great dining room. Interesting too, is the massive old fireplace, with its large iron cage or grate, capable of holding huge logs of wood fuel. Equally massive are the fire-iron holders, or 'dogs' as they are termed, which are splendid specimens, the iron-work being of the Elizabethan period. Early in the eighteenth century, the ten-

ants of the hall were a family known as the Kitsons, and it is to Miss Cecilia Kitson that we are indebted for the discovery of the old Latin Manuscript, from which our tale is taken.

Reading one winter night by the fire-glow in the great dining room, as she read her hand unconsciously reached out to the great crossbar of the iron dogs. The huge fire irons were not in their proper place, but had been, after use, merely thrown down on the hearth. Miss Kitson, holding her book in her left hand, began, as we have said, unconsciously playing with one of the iron dogs with her right hand.

Why she tried to turn it she did not know, or even why, when it moved, she kept on turning it, she could not tell, but she did, after several minutes of this turning round of the top bar of the iron dog, she felt herself being slowly, but most certainly moved along with the portion of the hearthstone on which she was cosily sitting in perfect obedience of the iron bar the whole frame of the massive fireplace moved forward. Astounded at the result, she still kept her nerve, and continued to work the hidden mechanism of the movable fireplace. When at last the handle would turn no more, she began to investigate the full extent of her discovery, taking care to lock the room door to prevent the entrance of possible talkative servants.

On either side of the cavity left by the moving hearth and fire grate, was room to penetrate behind and see what might be hidden there, for surely so elaborate and costly a mechanism must have had a purpose or use. Lighted taper to hand, Cecilia ventured behind the fireplace and found herself in a square room, perfectly ventilated, and fit for human habitation.

That it had been used was quite evident, chairs table, bed and all were there.

Still investigating her strange discovery, she drew the mouldering curtain off the bed, and as she did so it was with a great effort that she could keep herself from crying aloud in her surprise and terror, for there stretched upon the bed was a skeleton of a man, covered here and there with fragments of clothing that the slow process of decay still had left to mask, the variations in the time for the consummation of the inevitable end of all things mutable – 'Dust to dust' – 'Earth to earth' – still keeping her nerve, she took note of the various things in the secret chamber.

Her most important find, next to the body of the prisoner, was a closely written vellum book. This she brought away with her. Fearing discovery she left all else, and set to work again at the iron handle bar of the dog. With the reverse action the inner casing of the fireplace moved back again into its place.

Keeping her secret still to herself, she sat up all the night, and read the story of the man whose remains she had so strangely discovered in the secret chamber:

'The Catholic Invasion of England designed and carried out by the Society of Jesus, included many sons of the Holy Mother Church, who were, according to the ties of kinship, related to the great Catholic county families.

'Among these, I, Wilfred Howarth, was chosen for the work of God in the near neighbourhood of Rotherham, to wit, to make the ancient seat of my family, Howarth Hall, in the Canklow Meadow, the centre of my enterprise for the conversion of England. Here I came, and for a time was able to carry on active work for my church amongst my own people.

'Before my arrival, with the assistance of my uncle, Sir John Howarth, the famed engineer of the Tower of London drawbridge, the secret chamber doomed to be my burial vault was contrived, the whole of its hidden mechanism being made at Sir John's London foundry and secretly brought here and fixed by him, with such manual help as my father and brothers could render.

'Here for the expected time of trouble was a safe harbour or refuge, when the terrible persecution, religious and political, against our Holy Order did break out, it was only by using this safe retreat that I could escape arrest.

'In and around Rotherham the persecution of the Catholic families was bitter and persistent. Plots, many of them imaginary, some, alas, not so, against the Queen's life and her leading councillors, inflamed the public mind and many were the narrow escapes I had in the pursuit of my work and mission, the dire misfortune that brought me to the terrible end I now see to be mine.

'I herein record in the hope that some day when the record is found, my poor body may get Christian burial and that no needless mystery may cling to this hiding place of my necessity.

'The moving cause in my eventful story was the mad jealousy of a cousin of ours, Sir Hubert Vayne, of Tickhill Grange. He loved with a mad passion that would not brook denial, my sweet and beautiful sister, Elaine. Alas, for his peace of mind, Elaine detested him, preferring to espouse our near neighbour, Sir George Kennard, of Canklow House.

'This determination on her part to reject his suite roused the demon in his nature, and he set about his revenge in the most deliberate and persistent manner.

First he caused my aged father to be attainted as a Catholic recusant, on which

The old fireplace, behind which the hidden chamber was located. (Courtesy of Rotherham Advertiser*)*

charge he was put in bonds in Pomfret Castle. He knew of my activities and set many a trap to catch me, but I mercifully escaped his vile plotting.

'My brothers, Oswald and Edmund, were both charged by Hubert Vayne with connivance in the plot to place Queen Mary of Scotland on the English Throne, and so diabolically were his plans conceived that both suffered for a crime of which they were innocent. Only my sister, Elaine, remained, I dare not for a moment leave my hiding, so hotfoot were Vayne's emissaries on my track.

'Surprise and search parties in the Queen's name were almost of daily occurrence, yet my hiding place remained secure. Only two persons knew of its secret, my sister, Elaine and my uncle, the engineer, who planned and made it. There was one fatal flaw in its construction, and even that was thought an advantage, it could not be worked from the inside. Once imprisoned within, I had to wait until someone worked the secret mechanism without.

'Tracked one day by a company of soldiers to the very Hall itself, I had only time to get into my hiding, assisted thereto by Elaine, when Hubert Vayne strode into the room where my poor sister was seated making pretence of busy employ at her embroidery frame.

'Safe behind my prison walls I could hear what passed.

'"How now," said the villain, "Where is that Jesuit brother of thine?"

'"Where thou canst not hurt him, slayer of the innocent and renegade of thy family," was Elaine's spirited reply.

"'Tell me the priest's hole where he lies hiding, tell me without compulsion, or else I must use force."

"'Force, you will use force – brave Sir Hubert Vayne will e'en use force against a frail woman. Well bring hither thy thumbscrew or the toureque whipcord; they will all be apiece of the manner of the man who through spite of a girl, desolates her of her father and brothers."

"'I tell you I will find where he is hiding if I have to pull down the whole place and leave not one stone upon another."

'Then I could hear Sir Hubert sound the walls, panel by panel, he worked around the ancient wainscot, yet without the answering sound of suspicion. At last he grew tired and ceased his search, then evidently purposing further villainy he went from the room into the hall, where I could hear him dismissing the soldiery.

'I had just a moment to whisper a word of encouragement to Elaine through a cunning hole in the mantel, and then he returned.

"'I have told my men to take away your servants, all of them a tainted brood and now, Elaine, you and I must settle our accounts."'

The Hurried Horseman

Further sightings around this area have included sighting of a man on horseback galloping in the direction of where the famous hall once stood. Back in the 1960s, one of out website visitors recalls spending many an hour down there courting.

One summer evening, whilst parked in his car with his now wife, he heard the thundering of horses' hooves approaching the car from behind. Knowing that his car was blocking the path, he leant his head out of the window to check if there was enough room for them to pass. To his amazement, he saw a man on a black steed, wearing a tri-cornered hat with a riding cloak and boots, hurtling towards his car.

Fearing a collision, he embraced his girlfriend to shield her from the impact, only to see the horseman ride straight through his car and carry on towards the old abandoned hall. He never spoke of this frightening experience until he read our story on Howarth Hall.

Could this rider have been hurrying to the aid of Elaine?

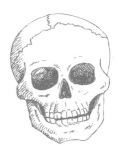

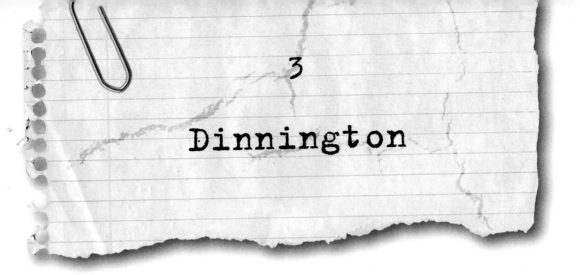

3

Dinnington

Tales from the Grave

In 1862, a barrow was discovered and excavated close to Park Avenue Road in Dinnington, Rotherham. A local archaeologist who worked at Oxford Museum at the time, returned home to supervise the excavation. The barrow was eight feet high and over forty-two yards long, and contained over twenty skeletons of people of all ages and both sexes.

Strangely, most were buried in a crouching position, but one figure was laid out with the head pointing north, and another that was unearthed was in the southern end of the burial chamber facing south. The remains seem to vary in depth as if buried at different times. The lack of artefacts on the burial mound itself led archaeologists to believe that the barrow was very old, as barrow burials ceased around the time Christianity became the predominant religion, which was approximately AD 627. Further tests revealed that the skeletal remains belonged to people of the New Stone Age, meaning that Dinnington must have been inhabited over 4,000 yeas ago, by the people who constructed the burial chamber. The skulls were placed in the Oxford Museum and today Clifton Museum, Rotherham, holds many of the artefacts unearthed.

During the late 1970s and early '80s, new houses were constructed on and around the site. Most of the barrow area was covered in woodland, and several of the new residents reported seeing what they described as being the walking dead wandering between the trees at night. This lasted for a number of years, bringing fear to the new-formed community.

Locals suggested that the excavating of the once hallowed ground had disturbed the resting spirits of the old barrow. Today sightings are rare; however, visitors still describe a strange atmosphere in the area, with only a few daring to walk their dogs in the vicinity after dark.

There's no Business like Ghost Business

Dinnington, near Rotherham, has a small theatre known as 'The Lyric', which was built in 1910 as a roller-skating rink. Later it became a Salvation Army Citadel until the Second World War, when it was used for dances. The building became run down and unused in the late 1950s and in 1962 Dinnington Parish Council purchased it and modernised the whole building.

The old theatre is thought to be haunted by one of its past stage. Conversations have been heard coming from what was once the dressing room, and even after trying the door, the voices continued until it was forced open, at which point the activity immediately stopped. Others have reported cold chills, lights flashing, and objects rolling uphill by themselves.

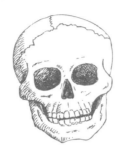

4

Firbeck

Phantoms of Firbeck Hall

Firbeck is a picturesque village on the outskirts of Rotherham which took its name from 'frith beck', meaning 'the stream in the woodland'.

William West was a lawyer and the son of Thomas West, of Beeston, Nottingham and Anne, daughter of William Bradbury of the Peak, Derbyshire. He made a fortune practicing law, and wrote a legal book called *Symbolaeographia*, for which he became famous. In 1594 he went on to commission the building of Firbeck Hall. His eldest son, William, succeeded him. John West, son of William Jnr, died in 1638, leaving a sister, Elizabeth, who first married Lord Darcy, son of Michael Darcy and Margaret Wentworth; and secondly, to Sir Francis Fane, who inherited Firbeck after her death.

Firbeck Hall estate was also held by the families of Knight of Langold, Gally-Knight and Stanyforth, until it was purchased by Mrs Frances Harriett Miles in the late nineteenth century. After the death of Gally-Knight the Firbeck estate, including the hall, was put up for sale in 1852 with the description:

Surrounded by beautiful gardens and pleasure grounds, with sheets of orna-mental water in the midst of park-like meadows, screened from the north and west by thriving plantations, and is approached by three lodge entrances. It contains upwards of 20 bedchambers with dressing rooms and water closets, entrance hall, billiard room, dining room, drawing room, library, vestibule and study, attached and detached servants offices, with noble vaulted and other cellars, there are cisterns on the top of the roof for hard, soft and river water. Upwards of 29 stables for horses with coach houses, carriage sheds, lofts, corn chambers and servants rooms.

On the death of Mrs Miles, the Firbeck estate formed the Miles Trust, which was inherited by Sydney Gladwin Jebb on the death of Henry Gladwin Jebb in 1898.

In 1935, Cyril Nicholson, a stockbroker from Sandygate, Sheffield, opened the hall as an exclusive country club known as Firbeck Hall Club. He had renovated it at a cost in excess of £80,000 and the hall now included a billiards room, ballroom, cocktail bars, restaurant and wine cellars. Other facilities included an eighteen-hole golf course, squash and tennis courts, swimming pool, aerodrome and stable.

The annual subscriptions were:

Full Membership: seven guineas
Ladies Membership: five guineas
Joint Membership: ten guineas
Country Membership (thirty miles): three
  guineas
Children or Wards of Members: from one
  to three guineas
Serving Officers of Army, Navy and RAF:
  three to five guineas

It is said that the club was patronised by the likes of the Prince of Wales. Rumour has it that he and Wallis Simpson used to frequent the club and the BBC would regularly broadcast dance nights from there. During the Second World War, the hall was used by Sheffield Royal Infirmary and the Royal Air Force, with the adjacent aerodrome becoming RAF Firbeck (opened in 1940 and used by 613 squadron). No. 659 Squadron formed on 30 April 1943 at Firbeck.

At the end of the war, the hall was bought by the Miner's Welfare Commission for use as a rehabilitation centre for injured miners. It closed in 1984, and became privately owned. In 2005, the grade II listed Firbeck Hall had been empty and decaying for more than a decade when thieves stole the lead from its roof, leaving the fragile building exposed to the elements.

The hall stands in its own landscaped grounds, containing a small lake, which was once used for fishing and rowing. As with most old houses, it has its share of ghosts. The most famous is the Green Lady of Firbeck Hall, reported to be the ghost of a young woman who threw herself into the lake and drowned.

It is uncertain if she was a daughter of a former owner, or a servant. However, rumour has it that at the outbreak of the First World War she was left behind by her fiancé, who had promised to return to her once the war

was over. He never made it back and the woman was left so grief stricken that she threw herself into the lake. Days later her body was discovered floating in the lake by the groundsman. It took three men to retrieve her body, as she was covered in pond weed. This is why she is known as the Green Lady.

Locals have often sighted the Green Lady, and say that the phantom rises from the lake, covered in pond weed, and proceeds to walk from her watery grave to the shore, with her arms outstretched and her clothes dripping.

A recent sighting came from a tradesman who was commissioned to carry out some remedial works to the building before it was purchased in 2005. He was working alone one day in the grand house, boarding up the windows and doors after a recent spate of thefts. Upon reaching the second floor he got the unnerving feeling that he was being watched and followed. Thinking this was the normal sounds of an old house settling, he started to whistle a tune to raise his spirits and take his mind off the unexplainable noises that surrounded him. To his terror his whistling was answered in kind as it finished off his well-known tune. Dropping his tools, he ran down the main spiral staircase and out through the old oak doors as a shriek of laughter echoed throughout the old halls and corridors.

A more recent sighting was reported in 2006, from a security guard working on the estate one summer's evening. He was sitting in his car on the driveway outside the main entrance next to the lake, with the window wound down and engine running, when he felt an ice-cold hand affectionately brush the side of his face. Startled, he turned to see what it was, only to be greeted by what he described as a young, lifeless woman in a long wet gown, covered in pond weed. Rigid with fear, he stared directly into her vacant eyes until she reached out and ran her freezing fingers down his forearm. With this he hit the accelerator and drove straight threw the padlocked gates, vowing never to return.

Other sightings have been seen on the third floor of the east wing, where the presence of an autistic child has been felt and seen following people through the corridors. It is thought that due to his disabilities, he was banished from public view and kept locked away in the attic for the remainder of his life. However, we have been unable to trace any records of a boy living there who fits this description.

Although we have only covered a few of its sightings, Firbeck Hall is thought to be haunted by a number of ghosts who have passed through its doors throughout history, some who may have died there during its time as a hospital or others who just return to visit the once famous Firbeck Hall Country Club. We only hope that Firbeck Hall doesn't fade into history like one of its ghosts.

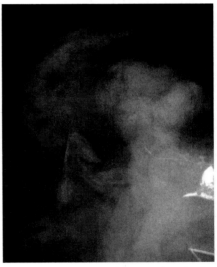

Right: This picture was taken by Joe late one evening at Firbeck Hall, the fog rising off the water seems to be in the shape of a young woman. (Authors' collection)

Below: The former Firbeck Hall Country Club as it stands today. (Authors' collection)

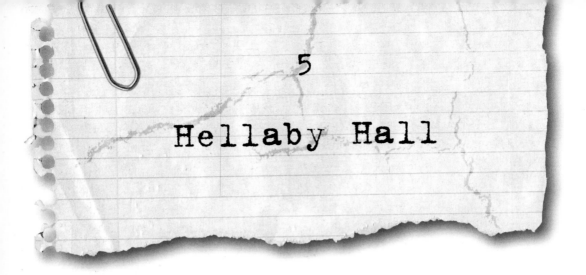

5

Hellaby Hall

HELLABY Hall was built in the late seventeenth century, around 1672, by Ralph Fretwell who made his money as the owner of sugar plantations in West Indies. The hall has an unusual Dutch Colonial gable frontage, reminiscent of the eastern countrys. Fretwell died in 1701. Samuel Clarke lived at Hellaby Hall in 1807 and was still there in 1824. John Clarke resided at Hellaby Hall in 1840, until at least 1848. Hellaby Hall was thereafter empty and derelict for many years. It was eventually bought and converted into a hotel, which opened in 1995.

Chaos in the Conference Room

Staff have reported that when arranging the room for a conference everything would be left neatly laid out ready for its delegates, but on returning to the room it would be disorganised and items such as pens, paper and glasses would be scattered all over the floor, even when staff had only been absent for a few minutes.

Windows to the Soul

A rather famous picture of Hellaby Hall was kindly submitted to us. It was taken by Jo Kay during the period when the hall was abandoned, before it was bought and opened as a hotel in 1995. A white figure can be seen in the centre of one of the windows.

The Late-Night Guest

At the main reception of Hellaby Hall Hotel, there have been several night porters unlucky enough to receive a late-night guest. They all report the same spectral sighting of a coach and horses entering the courtyard and then driving off out of sight, this is shortly followed by a man dressed in Victorian attire, who enters the lobby, not acknowledging them, and then vanishes into thin air, leaving the porter dumbfounded.

The Old Hag of Hellaby Hall

'Old Hag Syndrome' has also been reported at the hall. The 'old hag' type haunting is where the victims awake to find that they cannot move, even though they can see, hear, feel and smell. There is sometimes the feeling of a great weight on the chest and the sense that there is a sinister or evil presence in the room.

The name of the phenomenon comes from the superstitious belief that a witch – or an

What appears to be a ghost in a window at Hellaby Hall, prior to it being renovated. (Courtesy of Jo Kay)

Hellaby Hall, now converted into a hotel. (Authors' collection)

old hag – sits on or 'rides' the torso of its victims, rendering them immobile. The perplexing and very frightening nature of the phenomenon leads many people to believe that there are supernatural forces at work - ghosts or demons.

The experience is so frightening because the victims, although paralysed, have full use of their senses. This phenomena, as a rule, is accompanied by the sound of disembodied footsteps, a foul stench, apparitions of demonic figures, and the oppressive weight on the chest, making breathing difficult if not impossible. All of the body's senses are telling the victim that something real and unusual is happening to them.

The medical profession is aware of this phenomenon, but has a less supernatural theory than the 'old hag syndrome'. They call it 'sleep paralysis' or SP (sometimes ISP for 'isolated sleep paralysis'). Dr Max Hirshkowitz, director of the Sleep Disorders Centre, says that sleep paralysis occurs when the brain is in the transition state between deep, dreaming sleep (known as REM sleep for its rapid eye movement) and waking up. During REM dreaming sleep, the brain has turned off most of the body's muscle function so we cannot act out our dreams - we are temporarily paralysed.

The Old Woman of Room 5

The hotel boasts a large variety of rooms. Room 5 consists of a twin beds and on numerous occasion patrons have reported waking to the sight of an old woman standing at the end of the first bed as you enter the room, upon waking their room mate, the woman disappears.

The Homophobic Entity of Room 36

Room 36 seems to have an entity which doesn't like homosexual males; a hotel worker reported that on two separate occasions men have been attacked whilst sleeping in this room.

The first time this was reported was by a couple staying in the room. One of the men reported feeling paralysed and the sensation of being smothered by what he described as the evil presence of an old woman. This wasn't taken too seriously and was put down to a bad dream.

However, on the second occasion the incident was so bad that the two guests ended up sleeping on sofas in the hotel's foyer. They described the attacker as beingan elderly woman in her seventies wearing, a long black dress; she walked straight through the locked door and climbed on top of the bed before trying to strangle one of them. The victim had superficial bruising around his throat and wrists, which resulted in an official complaint being made to the hotel manager.

Many heterosexual couples have since stayed in the room without incident.

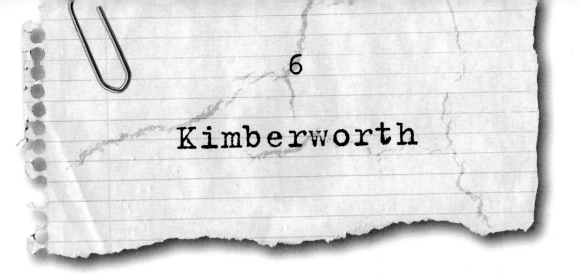

6

Kimberworth

Alpine Public House of Horrors

In the early 1970s a local woman was working as a cleaner at the Alpine public house, situated on Grayson Road, Greasbrough in Rotherham. It had recently been built and was modelled in the style of a Swiss cottage. A few weeks into her new job, the cleaner arrived early one morning and was stacking empty glasses on the bar, when she felt an icy chill run up her back. Turning around, thinking she must have left a door open, she was startled to see a monstrous, dark, hooded figure materialise in front of her, slowly advancing and trapping her between the bar and itself. The landlord, hearing her scream, came running down the stairs to investigate, only to find the cleaner curled up against the bar in a hysterical state, unable to tell him of her encounter.

From that day on, the bar staff started experiencing strange events and saw the same terrifying figure. This normally occurred when they were alone.

Around 1974, the landlord left and was soon replaced by a young couple with a small child. The new owners hired a barmaid to assist with the running of the bar. She was a local girl who had worked in other public houses in the vicinity, which was a great help as she was already familiar with the regular customers. The couple got on really well with the girl and asked her to double up as a babysitter on occasions to look after their daughter.

One evening the girl was babysitting and had been asked to spend the night, so the couple could stay out late and not worry about coming home. She put the child to bed and headed off to her own room to retire for the night. Soon after, she was awakened by the sound of the couple's dog, Rex, crying at her door. She got out of bed and opened it, thinking Rex wanted to be let out; he was quite anxious and proceeded to go down the stairs, stopping to ensure that she was following. It was obvious that he wanted her to follow him, but instead of heading towards the back door, he went towards the bar, but abruptly stopped dead in his tracks and refused to cross the threshold, now snarling and growling with all his fur standing on end. This was unusual because the dog was familiar with the pub and would often run in looking for crisp packets to tear apart.

The girl was shaken by Rex's behaviour and warily peered into the darkness. She

The Alpine in Kimberworth, Rotherham. (Authors' collection)

could just make out a grey mist forming in the middle of the bar, near the main light switch. Taking a deep breath, she marched towards the switch but, as she reached it, she felt an ice-cold chill before her. She turned on all the lights but could see nothing. Rex remained growling at the doorway and still wouldn't enter, even though the mist had now vanished. She went upstairs to the child's room, taking Rex with her, and locked the door until daylight broke.

The following morning she spoke of the night's events to the landlord, but he was not surprised by the story. He asked her not to mention the incident to his wife and daughter, because he too had experienced some strange happenings a few days earlier.

He explained that he had been walking down the stairs one evening to bring change for the till, when he felt someone, or something, pass him on the stairs which then was followed by a rush of cold air; this had unset-

tled him quite a bit, but he hadn't mentioned it as he didn't wish to frighten his family.

This strange phenomenon proceeded to occur throughout the years and subsequently the Alpine passed through many hands. This attracted a relief landlord with an interest in the paranormal, who had heard of the stories of the black-hooded figure. Intrigued by the urban legends surrounding the pub, it wasn't long before he allowed a friend of his to conduct a séance to try and solve the mystery of the supernatural entity. But tragedy struck. During the séance, while trying to make contact with the entity, his friend suffered a massive heart attack and was rushed to hospital by ambulance.

Horrified and disturbed by these events, the landlord decided he needed to take drastic action and requested an exorcism by the local priest.

Things seem to have quietened down since the exorcism, apart from the odd bump in the night.

Phantoms of Ferham House

Ferham House is also situated in Kimberworth, Rotherham. It was built in 1787 by John Platt of Rotherham. It became the home of the Habershon family in the 1880s and has been used for a number of purposes, including a single-mother's refuge and a workhouse. The home now holds grade II listed building status.

A report was made to us by a former worker that strange happenings had been taking place whilst they worked there. These included doors locking by themselves and windows slamming shut. There were also reports of furniture being seen physically moving and disembodied voices heard from empty rooms.

The most recent event happened several years ago to one of the staff members working there. She was walking down one of the corridors during twilight hours late one afternoon and was about to enter a room when she saw a tall man wandering around in a brown three-piece suit and wearing a flat cap. Not thinking too much of this, apart from his strange attire, she went about her business. She was discussing the strange man with a colleague later that evening, when her friend informed her that no men had visited that day and she must have imagined it. Adamant at what she saw, she went to check the visitors book and indeed found that no men had visited the building that day.

After this encounter, she started to enquire if others had seen such a man visit before, and was surprised to hear that one of the cleaners had also witnessed the strange figure one morning but was too scared to say anything in case of ridicule.

We have been unable to gain access to the building or any records associated with this grand house, but would be grateful for any information that could help identify who this distinguishing man is.

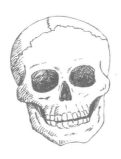

7

Laughton

Disappearing Coach

In the Middle Ages, Laughton was a thriving market town which drew custom from neighbouring villages. Its name is derived from the fact that it was a 'law town', a governing centre for the whole district.

The village suffered badly from the plague during this time and although some people survived the Black Death, a second type of plague hit the village which had a 100 per cent mortality rate. Some theorists believe that anthrax was the cause. The two plagues decimated the population and broke down the feudal system. This resulted in not enough people to work the land, and no landlords to ensure that vassals were 'kept in their place'. England was plunged into chaos, and by the time the population had found its feet again, feudalism, the system under which a landowner also 'owned' his tenants, was beginning to break down. Today Laughton is a small, rural village centred around a farming community, with very little evidence of its dark past.

Early one morning in the mid-1980s, a local man on his motorbike rode past the Gallows public house on his way to work in Thurcroft. The morning was quite misty, though it was not so thick as to make visibility too difficult. As he travelled along the road he began to slow down, as he could see an old-fashioned carriage, pulled by horses, heading in the same direction as him.

As he got close to the back of the carriage, he thought that it was unusual to see

The bridge where the horse and carriage was seen to disappear. (Authors' collection)

an outdated vehicle such as this, although he was aware that they were still being used for publicity purposes around the village and sometimes even for pleasure by local people. However, his interest turned to amazement as they drew close to the railway bridge. Instead of following the curve of the road and going over the raised bridge, the carriage carried on at the same level and drove straight into it, disappearing bit by bit!

Research showed that before the bridge was constructed over the railway, the road had indeed all been on one level. But at the time of the railway construction the road had to be raised at this exact point to accommodate trains which were to travel underneath. The ghostly carriage was evidently continuing along its original route!

The Gallows Public House

The Gallows public house marks the spot where villains were executed in Laughton as an example to the rest of society. Traditionally hangman's gibbets were situated on crossroads so that the spirit of the sinner could not find its way to the next world.

People would desecrate the bodies once hanged, normally at night to seek souvenirs such as the 'Hand of Glory'.

The 'Hand of Glory' was the right hand of an executed criminal, which was cut off while the corpse was still hanging from the gibbet. The blood was then squeezed out of the hand, it was embalmed in a shroud and then stewed it in a potion of saltpetre, salt and pepper for a fortnight. It was then left to dry in the sun.

The other crucial ingredient for its use is a candle made from the hanged man's body fat, wax and Lapland sesame. By placing this candle in the hand and lighting it, a thief could supposedly enter a house undisturbed, as it was believed that the Hand of Glory would cast a spell rendering the houses occupants into a state of comatose and thus allow the burglar to ransack and pillage the house at his leisure.

Thomas Ingoldsby (1788-1845), in his book *Ingoldsby Legends*, wrote the following verse:

> Wherever that terrible light shall burn,
> Vainly the sleeper may toss and turn;
> His leaden eyes shall he ne'r unclose
> So long as that magical taper glows,
> Life and treasure shall he command
> Who knoweth the charm of the glorious hands.

The Gallows pub is situated next to an old crossroads where Hangsman Lane passes. It is said that late at night you can still hear the noise of the hangman's rope creaking, as if a body is still hanging from the long-gone gallows.

However, the current landlord says he is not aware of any strange happenings in or around the building, despite the history of the place!

The Gallows public house stands on the site where the gallows would once have been. (Authors' collection)

8

Maltby

Roche Abbey

Roche Abbey, in the district of Maltby, Rotherham, was founded in 1147 by a Cistercian brotherhood who had travelled down from Newminster Abbey in Northumberland. Although they arrived in the valley in 1140, for several years they lived without a proper abode until the local lords offered to build them an abbey. 'Roche' means 'rock', and popular folklore has it that a vision of the crucifix appeared on a certain rock, after being struck by lightening, inspiring the monks to settle there. The image of the cross was so vivid that it was described as if it had been touched by the hand of God himself.

Although it has been said that no one was ever buried at Roche Abbey (because the monks were carried to Blythe Priory to be interred), there are a small number of graves belonging to local landowners who gifted money to the abbey in their lifetime, on the condition that, after their deaths, the monks would pray for their remorseful souls.

In 1534, Henry VIII ordered an investigation into all active monasteries in England prior to their dissolution. Roche was visited by the feared Doctors Leigh and Layton, who had the task of presenting a 'black book' of their findings to the king. Although Roche Abbey escaped closure at first, after being found to be financially viable, the success was short-lived because, on their second visit in 1537, Leigh and Layton reported that 'two-thirds of all monks there were drunkards and so bad as to defy description' so the abbey was closed. Leigh and Layton also reported that the monks were worshipping a nearby rock on which there was an image of the crucifix. If such a rock still survives, it must be deeply buried in the woodland which surrounds the ruins, and many have tried to locate this, but have been unsuccessful so far, including our good selves.

Fortunately, the monks were pensioned off peaceably. However, they still tried frantically to hide their pewter chalices in the woods, while the local people took hymn books and pews to repair their carts and wagons.

Old monasteries are often home to secret underground tunnels and 'priest holes', places in which to conceal people in times of religious uncertainty, when popes and abbots often opposed each other. The enclosed room was not always a safe one, so quick escape routes were felt to be the safest policy. Roche Abbey was no exception. There is still a network of underground tunnels beneath the abbey, leading to houses and castles in the surrounding area. Some of the tunnels run for miles, and have only been blocked off recently for safety reasons.

Towards the far end of the abbey itself, there lies a small stone coffin without a lid. Local legend has it that if one is to stare for long enough at the head of the coffin, then the face of the next person to die will appear. By whom the coffin was used remains a mystery.

The Haunted Abbey House

The Abbey House stands near the car park to Roche Abbey and is around 240 years old, although it appears much older. It was build as a hunting and gaming lodge for the wealthy and it is thought that the stone used to build this house came from the abbey ruins.

Locals recount seeing the spectre of a Grey Lady standing alone at one of the windows, staring out onto the grounds. The sound of a wailing child is said to have been

The Oracle Tomb, where the face of the next person to die is said to appear. (Authors' collection)

The Abbey today stands in ruins. (Authors' collection)

The house where the wailing child can be heard. (Authors' collection)

heard coming from one of the upper rooms, although on investigation the crying stops and the room is empty.

Visitors claim to have seen the ghost of a maid disappearing up a flight of stairs and legend has it that in the eighteenth century, a maidservant was made pregnant by a rich guest at the house, but shortly after her child was born, she killed the baby before hanging herself in the attic.

A New Year A New Sighting

In 1991, on New Year's morning, four visitors to the area reported seeing the spectre of a figure clad in white robes, gliding across the grass behind the hunting lodge towards them. The Cistercian Order who founded the monastery did indeed dress in white robes all year round. The face of the spectre was not visible, and it appeared to be moving at a great pace in their direction, shimmering with an unearthly, greyish light before disappearing out of sight at the remains of the old wishing well.

The area of grass it walked over was once the site of the wooden buildings which provisionally housed the monks and their abbey guests, until the stone structure was built.

Be Careful What You Wish For

Prior to Joe meeting Richard, he often went up to the abbey in search of the elusive spectral monks. One afternoon he called there with a colleague after finishing a building job in Maltby. He had a load of UPVC facia boarding and cladding fastened to the roof of his van when they pulled up in the car park. After paying to enter the visitor's centre, Joe explained the stories surrounding the abbey to his mate. His mate scoffed at the legends and began to mock them, purposely trying to provoke any spirits that may have been present. Joe, bemused at this, told him to stop as it was deemed unwise to mock the dead. Ignoring Joe's warning, he wandered off and sat down under the arches and waited for Joe to return.

Not long after this, it began to rain, so Joe met up with his mate and headed back to the van. Upon arriving they were stunned at the sight laid before them. The facia boards that were strapped to the van's roof had curled over into what he describes as 'being coiled up like the windings in an old clock'. Even his sceptical friend found it hard to rationalise how this had happened. After checking the cladding was still secure, they jumped back in the van and headed off up the cobbled driveway. Around halfway up, Joe said, 'See, I told you not to mock the dead, that's why the boards have bent over like they have.' His mate, knowing they were leaving, replied in a dismissive manner, 'Don't talk rubbish, it's just a coincidence.' At that moment the van's engine cut out completely and the vehicle began to roll backwards, forcing Joe to apply the handbrake. As the same time, the Rosary beads, that were hanging around the rearview mirror, snapped, scattering beads all over the van. Luckily, Joe managed to catch the cross before it fell. Joe's mate's smug grin had now been replaced by a look of sheer panic. Joe tried to start the engine a number of times, but each time the engine failed, until his friend finally apologised for his behaviour and at that the van started up and they got on their way. After this, Joe's mate couldn't get away from the old ruins fast enough.

Parking after Dark

We have received a number of reports from people who have witnessed similar phenom-ena in the abbey grounds; in one instance a group of friends went down in several cars one night after dark and were sat in the car park next to the old archways just outside the Abbey House. They were in the cars with the windows down and started sharing ghost stories with each other, the girls were screaming and messing around and the boys

The archways where the mist appeared from. (Authors' collection)

were elaborating the stories in a bid to scare them, when a low fog suddenly rolled in from under the arches and surrounded the vehicles. One of the witnesses described it as a scene from the famous horror movie *The Fog*. At this strange happening, the girls started to fret and wanted to leave, but the boys thought it was funny. Until, that is, a loud thumping and banging started happening on all the cars, causing them to sway from side to side, as if they were being attacked by a group of thugs trying to turn the car over. Scared, the whole group sped off from the scene, vowing never to return. Ever since then, the gates have been locked, to stop anyone parking there after hours.

9

Ravenfield

Ravenfield's (or Ranfield, as it was known until the nineteenth century) name comes from the term 'Raven's Open Land'. It is situated on the outskirts of Rotherham near the Doncaster boundary, and was first recorded in the Domesday Book (1086).

Today, Ravenfield is one of Rotherham's most picturesque villages, situated between Hooton Roberts and Bramley. The old village is to be found in a hollow below the Church of St James, close to the former site of Ravenfield Hall. In 1920 the estate was broken up and sold as farmland. Since then only thirty-five additional dwellings have been built.

Unfortunately, many of the old buildings have since disappeared, including Ravenfield Hall. Many local historical landmarks have also vanished from the area, such as ponds, ditches and wells which have been filled in, including what used to be the village's public well at the bottom of Church Lane. Most of the barns have now been converted into homes, whilst attempting to preserve their identity in design.

Fleeting Figure of Thrybergh Lane

This encounter was emailed to us by a lady who believes she experienced something paranormal back in the late 1980s. The following is her account of what happened:

> I am curious about ghosts but not really a believer. Although I had an experience about sixteen years ago when I saw what I believe was a ghost. I am very sceptical when people talk about orbs and I see pictures of alleged ghosts, I normally think they are all light anomalies or camera faults, but I know what I saw when I was driving down Back Lane at Ravenfield.
>
> I was heading towards Doncaster Road, near the bottom of the hill just as you come to the dip in the road where the graveyard in situated (clichéd I know) but something went across the road very fast, it appeared to levitate above the ground and I can only describe it as looking like a piece of black voile that had been blown across by a sudden gust of wind, even though there was no wind that night.
>
> I have never told anyone this story apart from my husband years later, whom

The entrance to the graveyard, where the fleeting figure has been seen. (Authors' collection)

then drove me to the graveyard in the daylight out of curiosity. Whilst there I never felt anything except a bit of unease at the thought that I could have seen the ghost of one of the people buried there. I still refuse to go there at night. As I say, I am sceptical of ghost sightings but I know what I saw and it has stuck with me ever since.

An additional witness sent us further information, adding substance to the story:

I am replying to the story in regards to a strange object which was seen on Back Lane heading from Ravenfield. Firstly, I would just like to say, you aren't the only one. When my boyfriend had just past his driving test we always used to park on that same hill at night and talk, so we could have our own space, before he would take me back home ... anyway, to the point.

We were sat in the car with the engine and lights off just talking, when all of a sudden we both saw the most strange black voile-type figure, which seemed to come from the left-hand side of the field across our path and vanish in front of the car. I myself have always thought 'I'll believe it when I see it' but I can now honestly say that I know exactly how you felt. We never said anything to anyone about it until years later, and then people just laughed at us, but we both knew what we saw that night and we never went back up there again.

What's strange about these two sightings is that they were witnessed years apart. We have been unable to identify what both parties saw whilst there, but please be careful when driving down this road late at night as this is known as an accident black spot. Maybe more people have seen this, but are afraid to report it.

The Scarecrow of Garden Lane

One summer's evening in 2006, a group of teenagers were driving down Garden Lane, towards Ravenfield Ponds. As they reached a spot where the road dipped, the figure of

The entrance to Garden Lane, where the 1980s man, or scarecrow, is seen. (Authors' collection)

a man dressed in 1980s clothing emerged. He was described as wearing a cream jacket and supporting a perm hairstyle. The group watched the man walk across the road in front of their car, causing the driver to break hard to avoid hitting him. The figure disappeared at the point of impact.

The group claim to have travelled this road a number of times since and have seen the man on many occasions, only for the same thing to happen each time.

Since this story was passed to us, additional sightings have been reported, but instead of the man been described as an '80s-type figure, he takes on the form of a scarecrow, still retaining his cream jacket, but with a hessian sack for a head. The witness account is as follows:

I was returning home one night with my friend after spending the evening in the Cavalier public house, Ravenfield. My friend suggested that we take a shortcut home back to Conisbrough via Garden Lane; he insisted that it would bring us out at the Hill Top Hotel. Not knowing the roads very well, I was driving cautiously when I saw what I thought was a normal scarecrow in the field to the right-hand side. Pointing this out to my friend we began to mock the effigy, what I saw then scared me half to death, the scarecrow turned and faced the car. Shocked, I screamed to my friend, 'did you see that?' He said, 'did that move?' We stopped the car to look at it again, only to see that it was no longer on its post. We panicked and set off at speed down the lane towards the woods, only to see the scarecrow type figure standing in the hedgerow of the field, staring directly at us. Terrified at this point, we turned the car around and set off back the way we came as fast as possible.

Whatever was seen late that night clearly didn't want people there! We have been unable to trace any recorded deaths on this road, and to date it remains a mystery as to the cause of the alleged haunting.

The men's terrifying journey started at the Cavalier public house.
(Authors' collection)

The road where the scarecrow stalked
its victims. (Authors' collection)

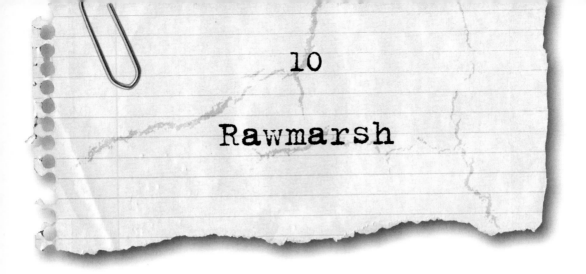

10

Rawmarsh

Comprehensive Ghost

Haugh Road Secondary School was built from red brick around the 1930s and consisted of two separate courtyarded buildings that housed boys and girls separately, whilst joined by a communal corridor and staff rooms. In 1967 planning permission was approved for the school to have additional buildings built at the rear, due to the increase in numbers of pupils at the school, and the name was changed to Haugh Road Comprehensive School. Today, further major improvements have been undertaken to bring the school up to a more modern standard, resulting in a change of name again, to Rawmarsh Community Sports College.

A report in a local paper stated that whilst the school was undergoing refurbishment work, one of the builders reported seeing what he described as 'a man who was about five feet six inches tall and dressed in a suit and was stooped over as if digging a small trench,' as the builder got closer, the man stood up and walked off through a solid wall. Stories of other strange happenings also emerged.

Rumours have it that the school could be built on an old burial site because it's situated right next door to the graveyard.

The school where the ghost was seen. (Authors' collection)

The Lady of the Seven Hills

The figure of a white lady has been witnessed running across the fields from the pit just off Greasbrough Lane, Rawmarsh, which is locally known as 'The Tops' of Seven Hills. She appears just after the highest point at the junction of Back Lane, where there is a spiralling blind bend as you descend down the hill towards the valley of the old railway line. This is a notorious accident blackspot.

She has been seen on numerous occasions by unsuspecting motorists, normally at dusk. They have watched the distressed woman scurrying over the crest of the hill just before the driver gets to the hairpin bend. Expecting to hit her on the treacherous turn, they slow down, only to discover that she has disappeared.

Witnesses have described her as being in her early twenties and wearing a long, white, flowing dress. Could she be trying to warn speeding motorists of the dangerous bend head? Or could she be the cause of the many fatal accidents that occur there?

'Aces Upon High' St Mary's Church

St Mary's Church at Rawmarsh is reputedly haunted by a pilot who lost his life in a plane crash in 1959.

Ian Wilson, who was nineteen years old at the time, was on a routine training flight in the area, when it is believed that his aircraft, a DH Vampire Jet trainer, developed technical problems. His remains were left there together with a family memorial until recently, when he was re-interred in the memorial garden in 2010.

The story goes that on that fateful day, Ian developed engine problems, and, fearful of hitting the church, he managed to head for the fields below the graveyard, where his plane crashed, killing him instantly.

At the time the church was in full service. Suddenly, the church doors were flung open and in walked a dishevelled young pilot, but before anyone could ask what he was looking for, he just disappeared in front of the congregation, leaving a stunned silenced. The silence was broken by an altar boy, who appeared in the doorway shouting for help and stating there was a burning plane wreck at the bottom of the graveyard. Most of the worshippers rushed to the scene to see if they could assist, but discovered that the pilot had perished on impact.

Over the years numerous reports have been made that a pilot fitting the same description is seen walking up the old cobbled path before disappearing at the church doorway.

Hit and Gone at 'The Whins'

Just before entering the village of Greasbrough from Neither Haugh is a road known as The Whins. This is the scene of one of the most inexplicable ghost sightings in South Yorkshire. There have been so many reports that even the police are aware of this long-standing sighting.

The point where the lady is seen to run towards the road. (Authors' collection)

St Mary's Church, Rawmarsh.
(Authors' collection)

The footpath where the airman
is said to walk up to the church.
(Authors' collection)

The usual scenario involves unsuspecting motorists being confronted by a jay-walking phantom, who hurls herself in front of oncoming vehicles, convincing the driver that they have taken her life in a tragic automobile accident, only for them to discover on inspection of the road that there is no one there.

Here are a few first-hand accounts of this particular haunting:

1970s Sighting

In the 1970s a local recovery driver was en-route to a vehicle that had broken down in Rotherham, accompanied by his young son, who was along for the ride. As they passed Wentworth East Lodge, they hit an old woman head on. The woman appeared in the middle of the road, wearing a dark cloak and carrying a basket; he stamped on the brakes but was unable to stop in time. As they hit the woman, she was hurled over the bonnet of the truck and all the fuses in the cab blew at the same time, leaving father and son in complete darkness. The driver got out of the cab and told his son to stay put, fearing what he would find. But he soon returned to the truck, stating that he couldn't find the woman. He fumbled with the fuses beneath the dashboard until he repaired the lights, so that he could search the road and look for the casualty.

He turned the truck around and frantically started to scan the road and hedgeways with the truck lights on full beam, but he was unable to locate her. Shocked and concerned for her well-being, he hurried to report the accident at Rawmarsh police station, where, after making his statement, the police informed him not to worry as this has happened before on lots of occasions and told him that the elderly woman was a well-known ghost!

1980s Sighting

In October 1980 a similar incident played out on an unsuspecting young man as he headed home from his girlfriend's house. At the exact same spot, just after Wentworth East Lodge, an old lady appeared in front of his car. Unable to stop in time, he hit the woman and she rolled over the bonnet, her face slamming against the windscreen. She stared right at him before hurtling over the roof and into a ditch. Horrified at what had just happened, the young man jumped out of the car and frantically searched for the body. After a distressing search, he was unable to locate her. Not knowing what to do, he drove home, where he broke down and told his mother the harrowing event.

She immediately contacted the police, who arranged to meet them at the scene of the accident. The police inspected the scene and the car whilst taking down his statement. Evidence of the impact was clear on the car bonnet; however, no body was discovered. Police continued their search until a senior officer arrived and asked the young man to give a description of the woman. He described the woman as being of a small frame and wearing a black shawl and cob hat. The officer paused for a while and then placed his arm around the trembling teenager and said, 'Brace yourself lad; what you just saw was a ghost,' and went on to explain that he wasn't the first person to have experienced such an episode on this stretch of road, for a number of other people had also reported hitting the mystery woman.

1990s Sighting

A man returning home one evening from a wedding in Wath, saw what he described as a little old woman dressed in black and carrying a basket, who appeared in front of his car. He swerved at the last minute to avoid hitting her, but was sure that he'd caught her with the front wing of his car. He jumped out and frantically searched the area, but was unable to trace her. Panicking, he telephoned his

The road where the old lady runs into the path of oncoming vehicles. (Authors' collection)

father, who lived nearby in Rawmarsh, and explained to him what had happened. His dad told him not to leave the scene and he would be with him shortly, and to try and stay calm. His dad soon arrived with his uncle to help, but their search was in vain.

While his uncle called the police, his dad discovered that the headlight on the left-hand side of the car had in fact been damaged, clarifying his son's story. The police soon attended, but were unable to locate the missing woman. The case was again dismissed, as no evidence of a casualty could be found.

Overview

It is rumoured that the spectre is that of an old gypsy woman who was trampled by a horse and buggy at this spot many years ago.

As you have heard, these reports span three decades and were already known to the police in the early 1970s. This sighting is so common that reports of a similar nature continue right up to the present day. If you regularly travel this route, then be sure to be on the lookout for the little old lady in black!

11

Rotherham Central

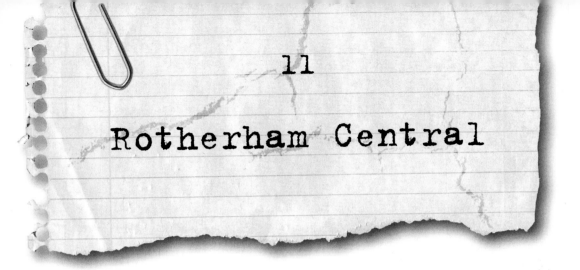

Little Boy Blue Coates Public House

The name of this pub recalls the building's original use as a charity school, known as the Blue Coat School from the uniform worn by the children. After 1547, the charitable work of the medieval guilds was taken over by the 'Feoffees of the Common Lands of Rotherham'. For the next 300 years, the Feoffees acted as a kind of town council. In 1708, they opened a charity school in a rented property until 1776, when it moved into a permanent building.

Staff working there today have reported the sound of a child crying, which they believe dates back to when the building was a school, also the sound of footsteps heard on many occasions throughout the building, and cold spots.

Seeking Refuge at Refuge House

Moorgate Road is one of Rotherham town centre's oldest roads, and contains a number of fine old buildings which were converted into business properties in the second half of the last century. Refuge House is one such building, and staff who worked there, prior to its renovation, witnessed a number of strange happenings over a period of several years. They frequently heard footsteps crossing the floors of the disused attic rooms, and witnessed doors opening and closing by their own accord.

In the early 1990s, a salesman was working late with a colleague in the main office at around 1 a.m. in the morning. They were just preparing to leave when, before their eyes, a stack of papers whipped up into the air and began to fly around in a whirlwind motion. They continued to circle for around for a minute before eventually fluttering to the floor. The two workers were stunned at what they witnessed and fled the building, leaving the papers strewn all over the office.

On a separate occasion, two other employees were preparing to lock up one night after

The Blue Coates public house in Rotherham. (Authors' collection)

Centre for injured ex-servicemen. During this period it was damaged by fire, and closed soon afterwards. Later, it was restored and converted into a sanatorium. Today it is still used by the National Health Service, as part of Rotherham District General Hospital.

The history of the building has been so varied that most people are not aware of its many uses throughout this century. In the late 1970s, a security guard was on his rounds one night when he saw a gentleman making his way towards him along one of the corridors. Concerned that security regulations were being breached. The guard approached the gentleman. As he walked down the long corridor he could clearly make out the dress of the intruder and described him as wearing a peaked cap and a long greatcoat. As they came within yards of each other, the guard could clearly see that he was a soldier dressed in a First World War uniform, with stripes on his sleeve. But before he had a chance to converse with the sergeant, the latter vanished into thin air.

The security guard ran away in terror and never returned to his post. Indeed, until several years after the incident, he had no idea that Oakwood Hall had once been used as a soldiers' rehabilitation centre.

Could this security officer's patrol have overlapped a sentry watch of a like-minded soul, who was also on guard that night?

My Children, My Children (Clifton Hall)

During the 1970s, the *Rotherham Advertiser* ran an article encouraging local people to report their paranormal experiences. One elderly Rotherham resident, Mrs Nettleship, recalled a strange sequence of events that happened to

ensuring that everybody had left the building, when they were stopped by a pitiful female voice pleading to them from upstairs: 'Please Sir, don't leave me! Don't lock me in!' this was followed by distressed crying that seemed to echo around the building. The two employees quickly fled the scene.

Our research showed that the upper floor of Refuge House was once used as servants' quarters when it was still a residential building. Could this have been the cries of a chambermaid who is still in residence today?

The Changing of the Guards at Oakwood Hall

Oakwood Hall, in Rotherham, was believed to be one of the grandest houses erected in the town in Victorian times. Businessman James Yates was an iron and steel baron, from Masborough, and in 1856 decided to build Oakwood Hall after making his fortune. He purchased Lawtons Farm and demolished it, before beginning the construction of Oakwood Hall on the land where it proudly sits today.

The hall was sold in the 1890s, and remained a family home until 1916, when work began to convert it into a Rehabilitation

her family in the 1930s, when they lived in a house on Clifton Lane.

The Nettleships had two young children, a baby boy and a four-year-old girl. Their circumstances then meant that the whole family were forced to share the same bedroom, a common practice at the time due to the economic depression.

Not long after moving in to their new home, the little girl started to show signs of distress when left alone in the bedroom, and pleaded for someone to stay with her because she was frightened of the white lady, who would appear wringing her hands and sobbing, 'my children, my children, where are my children?' Putting this down to vivid imagination, the Nettleships reassured their daughter that nobody could get into the bedroom, and told her it was just a nightmare.

Weeks later, while cleaning, Mrs Nettleship discovered an old-fashioned doll in a cardboard box at the back of the fitted wardrobe, which had previously been hidden from view on a high shelf. As the family was poor, she decided to keep the find a secret and repair the doll as a Christmas present for her daughter. She returned the doll to its hiding place, pleased with her find.

On the same evening of this discovery, at around 9.30 p.m., the Nettleships were in the living room when they were startled to hear a piercing scream coming from upstairs. They raced up to the bedroom and were unable to find their little girl, until they heard a rustle coming from the wardrobe. Opening the cupboard door they found her, nightdress torn, cowering in the corner. Her mother immediately embraced her and took her downstairs for comforting. Later, she described her daughter as being 'rigid with terror'.

The girl described how the white lady had tried to take her away, and she'd had to

struggle to pull away from her. Although the Nettleships could see for themselves that their daughter was in a terrible state, they dismissed the story as a vivid nightmare. However, as time progressed, she became more and more subdued and reclusive and even stopped eating, eventually becoming ill.

Mrs Nettleship took her daughter to the children's clinic, where the doctor informed her that somebody − or something − had obviously frightened the little girl very badly for her to be in such a state of terror. He went on to describe how she was showing similar symptoms to soldiers returning from the front line, who had suffered from shellshock. The Nettleships once again put this down to the 'nightmares' which they assumed she had been having, since their son (who slept in a cot next to her) had never once been disturbed.

Shortly afterwards, the family decided to move house due to their daughter's ill health and nightmares, but before they left, Mrs Nettleship went to look for the old doll she had found some months previously in the wardrobe. The box was exactly where she had hidden it, but the doll had vanished from inside. Confronting her husband about its whereabouts, he recounted that he had looked in the box the day they had moved in, but said there was never a doll inside.

Was it a phantom doll at Clifton Lane? (Authors' collection)

Although the strange events on Clifton Lane were never quite forgotten, the family moved on with their new life and soon the memories faded into the past, until, many years later, an article in a Rotherham paper caught Mrs Nettleship's eye. The piece was about local ghosts, entitled 'The White Lady of Clifton Hall'. Mrs Nettleship was horrified to read that the self-same White Lady is said to appear wringing her hands in distress as she cries for her lost children. Mrs Nettleship began to believe, for the first time, that perhaps somebody – or something – could indeed have tried to take her young daughter away.

Research into the history of Clifton Hall showed that it was opened as the Rotherham Volunteer Drill Hall in 1873. From about 1910 the hall was used for concerts and film shows. After the Second World War it ceased to be used by the Royal Volunteers and was renamed 'Clifton Hall', coming under the control of the local authority. Attempts were made to turn it into a nightclub and disco in the late 1980s, but the appropriate licenses were never granted, forcing the council to put it up for sale. However, due to lack of interest by perspective buyers, they demolished it in 1991 to make way for a car park.

The origin of these hauntings remain a mystery today …

Mysterious Midget of Moorgate

In the 1800s, a chapel was built in Rotherham on Downs Row by a local minister. Today, you would never know that the chapel still stands due to it being hidden by the properties on Moorgate, but it looks just as good as it would have done back then. However, it is now used as a business dwelling instead of a place of worship. But in the gardens surrounding the building there are still the tombstones of the people who were once buried there.

The following story was submitted to us after an appeal was made for local sightings in the Rotherham area:

In 1969 I was a probationer constable in the Sheffield and Rotherham Police. On my first shift I was accompanied by an old sergeant who, whilst we were walking along Moorgate, introduced me to a man called Bob Moodle. Moodle had been an old-timer when my sergeant was starting out, so Bob must have been a copper in the 1920s/'30s. When he had gone, the Sergeant told me a story of how Moodle had one night been having a smoke at the rear of a small chapel off Moorgate (still there, behind the monumental masons shop), he was stood in the chapel graveyard, when, from behind a gravestone, a dwarf dressed in a top hat jumped out, knocked his helmet off, and attacked him! Moodle ran all the way back to the old police station on Frederick Street. He reported it to colleagues, who knew of the story but didn't believe it. He served for many more years in Rotherham and had a distinguished record. However, he always refused to work Moorgate beat at night.

I worked Moorgate beat for a number of years and often went for a fag in the chapel graveyard. Whilst I was aware of the story I often felt drawn to the place and was never afraid until one night in about 1974. I was stood in the chapel yard, looking out over Canklow, when I

Downs Row, where the chapel is situated. (Authors' collection)

who was in fact the son of the minister who built the church, and was buried in the same grave as his mother and father, so his name was never engraved on the tombstone. This is not to say, however, that there was never a plaque or tombstone in his memory.

Below is the information we received on the above story:

heard a noise behind me. Turning around, I caught sight of a very small man walking out of the graveyard and along Downs Row towards Moorgate, he appeared to have a stove pipe type hat on, similar to Moodle's reported attacker all those years ago. Aware of his story, I cautiously followed and was around ten feet away when he turned into Moorgate. As I also turned the corner, I was astounded to see that he had vanished. I did not take the matter further as I was about to resign from the police service and did not want the hassle.

Whether what I saw was my imagination running wild, I don't know, but I had been down to the chapel yard numerous times and had seen nothing. All I know is that the man walked from the direction of a gravestone that bears the inscription 'Lord Billy Lee erected by his friends from the circus'.

After looking into this story in more detail, we were unable to locate the gravestone or records of any such person of that name being buried there. However, we received additional information from an anonymous person, who clarified that there had actually been a man buried in the churchyard of that description,

The chapel is on Downs Row and was rebuilt by my third grandfather removed in the 1800s. He was also minister there for forty-three years. His gravestone overlooks Canklow, which has been described. On his gravestone is inscribed with himself and his wife. But, there is another in the grave that is not on the headstone. This person is their son and who measured 3ft 3in and was thirty-five when he died. He was quite a character as most people in Rotherham knew him as he had a stationers shop on the High Street. Unless the persons who saw him had read a very rare book which I own, no one knows he is there.

The graveyard where Moodle was attacked. (Authors' collection)

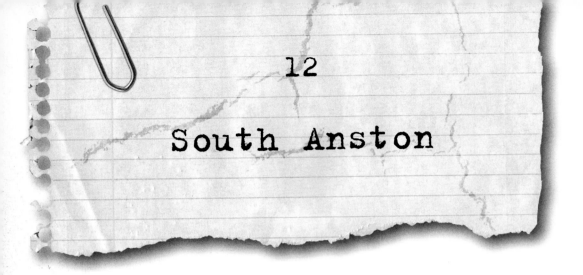

12

South Anston

Creepy Cottages of South Anston

South Anston is an old farming village dating back hundreds of years that mainly consisted of small cottages that were once tenant farm buildings. However, today it's a thriving village on the A57, with modern housing and schools which have been built around the once small hamlet.

Near the Norman church is a path that leads to a row of cottages which have been standing throughout this time. In the 1990s, one of these cottages was in the process of being renovated into shared accommodation. An old man stopped and leaned on the garden wall before moaning to the workmen, 'I wouldn't buy that house for love nor money.'

'Why?' asked one of the builders, slightly annoyed.

'It's haunted to bloody hell,' replied the old man, before walking off.

Remembering his warning, they conveyed this to the new owner, but he dismissed it as the ramblings of an old man.

Once the work was complete, the landlord soon moved his new tenants – two young students – in. All seemed well until one morning, when one of the girls came down stairs and saw an old man standing at the window hanging curtains. Thinking he was a handyman sent by the landlord, she shouted from the kitchen 'would you like a cup of tea?' Not getting a response from him, she went into the room to discover that he had vanished. Thinking he'd gone outside to get some tools, she went to the door, only to find that it was bolted from the inside.

Later that week, her flatmate saw the old man again. He was sitting in a chair, smoking a pipe, before suddenly disappearing. In addition to this both girls reported the smell of pipe tobacco on numerous occasions in the living room, despite neither of them smoking.

Due to the strange happenings, the turn over of tenants was high. New occupants weren't told of the hauntings, but within days of them moving in they became aware of a strange presence. The new tenants put this down to the property being old, but soon fell victim to bad luck and a feeling of depression and despair. Anyone brave enough to stay any length of time began to suffer from these symptoms and became withdrawn.

Many tenants reported that timepieces had a habit of stopping, and then resetting themselves back to the correct time, with no aid of human intervention.

Two tenants were sitting in the large room at the back of the house one night when suddenly the wall light went off. Both turned to look at it, and watched in amazement as the bulb unscrewed itself out of the light fitting before flying across the room and shattering against the wall. The tenants left soon after this frightening event.

Eventually, word got around that the house was indeed 'haunted to bloody hell' as forewarned by the old man, making it difficult to let the rooms. So the landlord had no option but to take up residence there himself. It didn't take long for the property to begin to take its toll and he himself experienced a run of bad luck and depression as the house consumed him. Subsequently, he put it on the market, but found it difficult to sell.

Rumours later emerged that the hauntings were the result of a man said to have been plagued by voices before putting his head in the oven and gassing himself in the kitchen of the old house. However, the house is today occupied by a new owner and the hauntings seemed to have stopped.

Within walking distance of this property is another stone cottage, built around the same era, which stands proudly next to the old Norman church. In the 1970s, this was purchased by a young couple as a renovation project. Excited at their new venture, work was quickly underway.

During the renovation work the couple were forced to live upstairs whilst the work was carried out. One evening, whilst having a strip-wash in the sink, the husband felt something grasp hold of him on the right shoulder. He described this as being grappled by a cold, clammy hand and it was with such force that it made him wince. Spinning around to confront his aggressor, he was surprised to see

that there was no one there. Not wanting to alarm his wife, he kept the unpleasant incident to himself, but little did he know that this was just the start of things to come.

Not long after this, both he and his wife heard the distinctive sound of large, heavy chains being dragged across the rear courtyard. This puzzled them, as the courtyard was full of rubble and, after investigation, no explanation for the sound could be found.

Several weeks later, the couple were called by the builders to come and look at what they had uncovered. As they were knocking out the alcoves to the chimneybreast in the living room, they had discovered a secret L-shaped passage that lead to a chamber behind the old stone fireplace. To their horror it housed a stone coffin. Freaked by the gruesome discovery, the couple instructed the builders to remove the coffin immediately. However, due to the size and weight, the coffin had to be smashed to pieces to be excavated. The builder said that the chamber must have been built around the sarcophagus, due to its size. What's strange about this story is that the couple's dog had been growling at the wall where the coffin had been discovered on a number of occasions prior to the wall being pulled down.

Many other strange occurrences happened after this, including disembodied footsteps heard walking across the floor above the living quarters, and a door bolt unlocking, the door opening and revealing no one there.

Once the work had been completed on the property, things seemed to calm down a little, and the couple began to accept the strange noises as the norm. One summer's day the husband was digging the garden, ready for landscaping, when he uncovered a human skull. Amused by this, he took the skull into the house to show his wife, who screamed at his find and insisted they called the police. Within the hour the police had arrived and cordoned off the garden. Excavations uncovered a second skull and the remains of two bodies in a shallow grave. Forensic tests later dated the bodies as being over 400 years old.

No records for the bodies could be found, but experts believe that the cottage could have once been a chapel of rest for the Norman church. Criminals were forbidden to be buried on consummated ground, and it is thought that they were interned here under cloak of darkness by sympathisers, so that their final resting place was on holy land.

The family still live in the property and report that activity is ongoing. However, they have learned to live with it and have no intention of moving away.

It is not known if these two properties are linked in any way; however, it does seem strange that both have experienced a large amount of paranormal activity within such close proximity to each other. Maybe it's not the cottages that are haunted, but the area as a whole. We would be interested to hear of any other similar reports from South Anston.

Aston Stones

Anston Stones is visible as a belt of trees on the A57 between Sheffield and Worksop, and

The entrance to the wood where Anston Stones are situated. (Authors' collection)

has an unusual history, which dates back to the Ice Age. Many artefacts of interest have been found, ranging from flint arrow heads to Roman pottery. It is also said to have been used in the Robin Hood era as a smuggling route.

The Legend of the Boggard

The name boggard is used to describe a troublesome ghost or spirit, very much like poltergeist. It is related to barghast, from the German *geist*, meaning spirit or hell hound creature. They are said to be silent in motion, about the size of a calf, with a shaggy, black coat. They exude a distinctly sulphurous smell and their crimson eyes glow like fire. Although appearing to be solid, they can disappear at will, sometimes in a fiery explosion. If anyone is foolish enough to touch a boggard, death will strike them shortly afterwards.

By tradition, the boggard materialises to forewarn of death or disaster. The apparition of a black dog often occurs near burial grounds, and to see the animal means impending death for someone nearby.

The nature of this haunting is similar to the banshees of Irish folklore. These apparitions of wailing women are said to be heard by family members when a death is imminent. It is normally a relative or close family friend of the person who sees the phantom who is the target.

Traditionally, newly consecrated burial grounds were designated a guardian in the form of a black dog; it protected the dead from the Devil, demons and other nefarious supernatural creatures. The dog was often seen on stormy nights and was regarded as an omen of death.

It was believed in the past that the first burial in a churchyard would have to watch over the rest of the dead. A dog must be buried first before a human. To do this they would sacrifice a large black dog and bury it in an unmarked grave in the furthest corner of the graveyard, so that its spirit would guard the consecrated land and prevent the dead rising from the grave.

Sometimes black dogs/boggards can appear at the scene of a murder or suicide. They are frequently reported to appear at crossroads, where witches were buried. It was traditional practice to bury a purported witch who had been executed at a crossroads, so that their soul could not find its true path and they would be lost forever, thus preventing their soul from seeking revenge.

Superstitious miners frequently connected certain accidents with the sighting of black dogs. If a miner saw a black dog on his way to work, he was to turn around and go back home. This was a sign that something bad about to happen.

Boggarts and barghasts appear all over the Peak District and South Yorkshire, most famously in Boggards Lane in Sheffield.

Sightings of the Boggard in Anston

A man from out of the area was spending a short holiday with a friend in North Anston, in the summer of 1993. The weather was fine

A boggard. (Authors' collection)

and warm, and the friends decided to go for a walk through the woods towards Anston Stones. They reached one of the many rocky outcrops about half a mile into the expanse of green belt land, when the man decided to go on ahead and climb to the top of a small crag. As he was walking in between two columns of rock, he felt curiously uneasy, as though he was being watched. Undeterred, he found a foothold and began to climb the rockface. He reached the top and was astonished to see a huge black dog, about one and a half metres tall, with glowing red eyes and the physique of a Rottweiler, standing approximately ten feet away from him.

The dog stood motionless and stared, howling. The man remembers feeling as though he was not witnessing an 'earthly' event, and described how his blood ran cold, as a sudden chill came over him. He climbed back down the rockface as quickly as he could and called out to his friend, who was standing below, 'Did you hear that?'

She had seen and heard nothing, and quickly ran around the crag and up to the area where her friend had been startled by the black dog. There was nothing there; no trace of a dog, or a person who could have been walking such an animal. They searched the area thoroughly, but there was nowhere for a dog of that size to have disappeared so quickly without trace. The pair retraced their route and left the scene, whereupon the temperature appeared to return to normal.

Although the most rational explanation would be that the hound was not a phantom at all but an ordinary domestic dog, the man to this day remains unconvinced and described his encounter as a 'once in a lifetime experience', and has refused to return to Anston Stones on subsequent visits to South Yorkshire.

Adding credibility to this story was another sighting of the black dog, also seen in the winter of 1993 by another witness, this time

at the bottom of the crag in the dead mans cave. The man heard the sound of whimpering coming from within, approaching the entrance with caution he looked into the darkness, thinking that it was an animal in distress, only to see the boggard manifest itself with white snarling teeth and burning ruby eyes, scaring the unsuspecting hiker half to death. Coiling into the foetal position he closed his eyes and awaited his fate, but nothing happened. When he re-opened his eyes the beast had gone!

The Dead Man's Cave

One of the more famous parts of Anston Stones is 'dead man's cave', also known as 'hermit's cave', after a local man, who lost his fortune through drink after losing his wife to an unknown illness. He took up refuge in the cave and became known locally as the hermit. Stories reveal that the hermit lived there for many years, away from the rest of the village. The villagers would warn their children not to disturb him, claiming that he was normally drunk and abusive to anyone who would venture near his cave.

Little is known of the hermit due to his living in the cave, undisturbed, for many years, and it was some time before anyone found his decomposing body. It is claimed that his spirit still wanders the cave, as people have reported seeing a tramp-like figure appearing near the entrance of the cave.

A local man from Dinnington, situated about two miles from Anston Stones, reported that in late 2005, he was walking through the woods with two friends when they stumbled upon the cave.

They climbed down the steep cliff face and headed towards the lime stone opening. He began to tell his friends of the local legend of the hermit, but they didn't take much notice of his comments. All of a sudden a bright flash of light blinded the group and struck them dumb.

The cave where the hermit has been seen. (Authors' collection)

Shocked by what they had just experienced, they scrambled in terror back up the cliff face, anxious in case the incident happened again.

As they neared the top of the niche they looked back over their shoulders, and were horrified to see the figure of an old man in a long greatcoat and a tall, black hat lumbering at an increasing pace up the crag behind them, way too fast to be of this world. The figure got within feet of the last member of the party as he ascended the summit of the crags. Turning around, he peered into the face of the apparition and was mortified to see there were no features.

Running through the woods, they stopped and looked back to see if the hermit was in pursuit, only to watch it rear up to its full height and dematerialise into thin air before their very eyes.

Our advice regarding Anston Stones is to remember this childhood fable:

> If you go down into the woods today, be sure of a big surprise ...
> If you go down to the woods today, you better not go alone.
> It's lovely down the woods today, but it's safer to stay at home ...

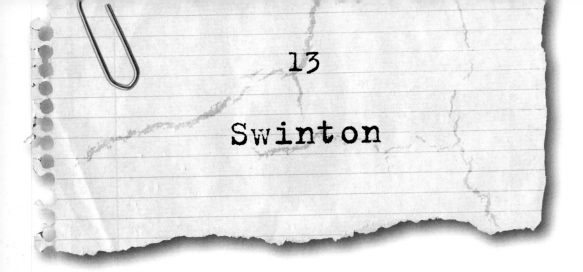

13

Swinton

The Glass House Ghost

Brothers Thomas and Charles Hattersley moved to Swinton from Sheffield in 1864. They went on to establish a large and prosperous industrial enterprise on Whitelea Road called Queen's Foundry. A wide range of manufactured goods were made, including many types of domestic and industrial heating equipment and home appliances. The works had an impressive record of entering their products in national trade and industrial fairs. The heating industry is still manufacturing in Swinton at the Stelrad Plant.

Swinton was home to the glass industry from the 1850s until 1988, trading under a number of names, including South Yorkshire Glassworks, Dale & Browns, Canning Town Glass and United Glass Containers. The former Queen's Foundry on Whitelea Road was bought by United Glass during the 1980s.

The foundry building is reportedly haunted by a former employee who died in a tragic accident there some time ago. This story was passed on to us by an ex-workmate of Joe's, who was working for a local security firm at the time.

Just before the Queen's Foundry was refurbished into the Hattersley building, as it is known today, security was required to protect the new windows and fittings whilst they were waiting for new tenants to move in. The guard's duties included an hourly patrol and manning the main reception desk, making sure that all visitors logged in and out in the visitor's book.

Shortly after one of these patrols, the security guard was returning to the reception desk when he saw a man dressed in brown bib and brace overalls walk past his desk and into the gents' toilets. At first he thought this must be a contractor viewing the building, so followed him in to ask him to sign the visitor's book. As he opened the door, he saw the man with his back to him. The guard said, 'Excuse me mate, but you need to fill in the visitor's book before you're allowed in here,' but when the man turned around, the guard was horrified to see that he had a mangled torso and face, and was almost unrecognisable as human. They stood face-to-face for a moment before the apparition disappeared. The security guard was so shaken, that he took ill and had to be relieved of his post.

The guard didn't return to active duty for several months, but by the time he returned no other sightings of the ghosts had been

The Queen's Foundry today. (Authors' collection)

reported by his colleagues, who worked there after him. However, the legacy left other guards in fear of working there alone.

Stories emerged later that a former worker had been carrying out repairs when he was caught by an overhead crane. The noise of the machinery was so loud that no one could hear his cries for help, until it ripped the poor fellow apart, before carrying his body through the factory, leaving a trail of blood.

We have tried to find records of an accident of this type taking place here, but to date have been unsuccessful. Could this spectre be the ghost of this tragic worker, or is this just another urban legend told by nightwatchman?

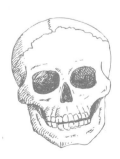

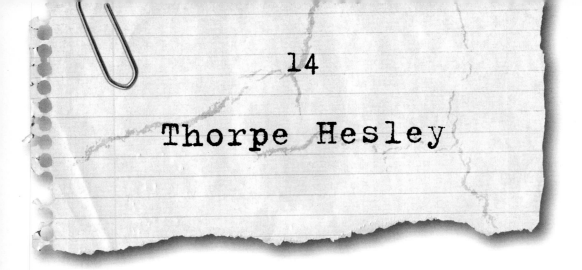

14

Thorpe Hesley

Haunted Hesley Woods

Bordering the Wentworth estate is Hesley Woods at Thorpe Hesley, which is renowned locally as being haunted by a number of spectres.

Many sightings have been reported by people camping there at night or taking walks during twilight. The following story came from a group of teenage boys who spent the night in the woods during the summer of 2008.

The night was quite light and they were camping down near the bridge when they witnessed what they describe as a black-cloaked figure moving at great speed towards them. One of the eyewitnesses described the spectre as gliding across the ground as though it was skating on ice. But what was most disturbing was that the figure was elevated about two feet above the ground and silent as it moved.

The boys, who at first were frozen to the spot in fright, soon regained their composure and turned on their heels when it got within twenty yards of them, and ran at full pelt out of the woods. Quite shaken at what they had all witnessed, they only returned at daybreak to retrieve their belongings.

Other reports have been made by people while out walking their pets and normally consist of strange shapes appearing along the hedgerows, as if someone is stalking them. Upon stopping, disembodied footsteps can still be heard, as though an invisible entity is present. This strange feeling of being observed is also accompanied by odd light formations and the smell of sulphur.

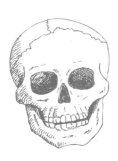

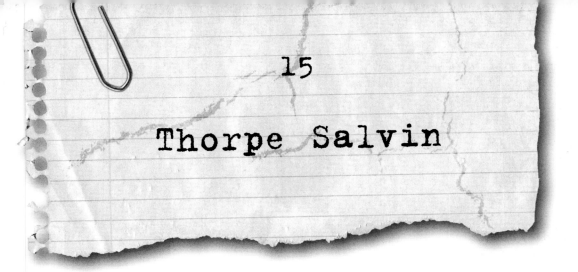

15

Thorpe Salvin

The Manor Ghost

Thorpe Salvin is a historic village situated a short distance from the north Nottinghamshire border, boasting the ruins of an Elizabethan square-style manor. Thorpe Hall was once a quadrangular house with circular turrets at each corner, but today stands in ruin.

There are stories of a mysterious figure which has been seen walking in between the empty windows of the remaining walls. A silhouette is said to appear on a brick outcrop by the light of the moon. When viewed from the road at night, at first glance the building appears to be an entire manor, until you step closer and find only the front wall intact. It seems that no family was ever comfortable here for long, and within a short space of time the building fell into ruins.

Even though Thorpe Salvin was a small village, it did not escape the conflict of Civil War in the seventeenth century. The parish register records that five men were buried in one October there, after being slaughtered in a fight on Thorpe Moor with the garrisons of Welbeck.

Based near Worksop was a garrison of Parliamentarians, and in a clash with the Welbeck Royalists, who had drawn some of their number from Thorpe Salvin, the Parliamentarians killed five men and forty were taken prisoner. Luckily, one man escaped, Thomas Battersbie, but they severed his hand and it was buried in the churchyard at Thorpe Salvin, this later created the rumours of a phantom disembodied hand seen there.

Packman Lane

The village of Thorpe Salvin is separated from Harthill by an ancient highway, now called Packman Lane. This lane was one of the oldest trade routes in Britain – it is thought that it even dates back to Roman times – and hundreds of years ago was worked by the notorious 'Thorpe Salvin Highwayman'. This stretch of road has become the location of numerous ghostly sightings.

The Thorpe Salvin Highwayman

Drivers have reported that, when driving down the well-known dip at night, their headlights illuminate something strange in the dip in the road. The description is that of a flash of a silver stirrup or, on occasion, a sighting of a man on a black horse hailing the

What is now left of Thorpe Hall's grand hall, where the ghost sightings have been seen. (Authors' collection)

The dip in the road where the highwayman holds up motorists. (Authors' collection)

vehicles as they pass. He is said to be dressed in a dark cape and a tricorn hat, his face is covered with a black handkerchief. As soon as the vehicle headlights shine away from the figure, he can no longer be seen. Almost as if the car's headlights are illuminating him onto the bank of fog that sits in the dip, a bit like a projector in a picture house.

In 1991, unsuspecting motorists witnessed the bandit. As they drove into the dip, the headlights lit up what appeared to be a highwayman brandishing a pistol and beckoning them to halt. He rode directly across their path into the neighbouring hedge, and, as soon as the headlight no longer illuminated the bank of fog, he disappeared. They decided to turn their car around to see if they could see it again. Every time they were heading towards Thorpe Salvin the figure would appear in the same place at the side of the road, before vanishing again as the car travelled up the hill.

The highwayman's ghost seems to be triggered by the approach of headlights. Many wonder if he thinks these are the lamps of old stagecoaches that he once robbed by night.

Local legend suggests that a highwayman was caught close by and was hanged, leaving his body to rot on a gibbet in Thorpe Salvin, warning other potential highwaymen of their fate should they try to commit the same type of deed.

The Roman Legion

Strange as it may seem, and centuries apart, there have been other reports of an apparition, this time a Roman legionary, who is said to walk along the road from time to time heading towards Thorpe Salvin. He is described as wearing a leather skirt, a breastplate and iron helmet, and normally appears at dusk to unsuspecting motorists driving alone down the lane.

During our research for this book, we went to Packman Lane to investigate some of this phenomenon. Whilst there, several people stopped, thinking we were in need of help due to its remote location. Upon explaining our reasons for being there, we were surprised to hear that they had also seen the unexplainable figure crossing the road at night. We have visited the road on numerous occasions but have yet to witness the highwayman or Roman legionary for ourselves.

An illustration of the Roman legionary. (Courtesy of Rotherham Library)

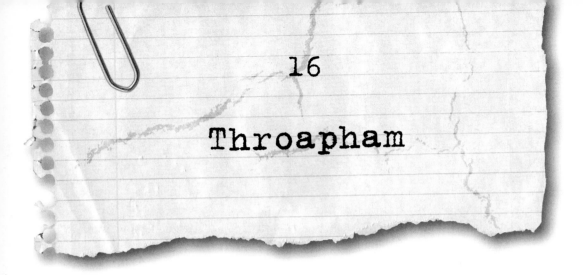

16

Throapham

The Lady of Throapham Manor

There once was an old manor house in the hamlet of Throapham, near Dinnington, but it was demolished at the beginning of this century. At one time, Throapham manor was a focal point for local fox hunts, and even boasted its own special breed of horses which worked the land surrounding it.

Many residents know of the ghost of Throapham, which still haunts the once grand estate. Reports have been made by locals that, around autumn time, she walks from the site of the former manor house, down the path to the orchard, before disappearing at the foot of an old tree. She is described as a young woman wearing a long, green gown, with raven black hair.

Pupils at Dinnington Comprehensive School, whose cross-country course runs through Throapham wood, still fear the thought of confronting 'The Lady of the Manor' whilst running the route. Children now name this part of the route 'Running the Gaunlet'.

Signpost to the village of Throapham, where the manor once stood. (Authors' collection)

The Ghost that Likes the Dark

Throapham sits on the edge of Dinnington, off Old Coates Road, and boasts a selection of old buildings that were originally farm cottages and stables. One of these homes has experienced a number of bizarre events, deemed to be poltergeist activity.

A young couple moved into one of the renovated cottages and soon began to feel the sensation of being watched. Putting this down to an over-active imagination, and the building being old, they tried to get on with their lives. However, further events soon started to take place, as if a mysterious presence was sharing their home with them.

One evening, when the couple were in the living room, they heard an unusual noise come from the hall, which sounded like a champagne cork popping followed by the sound of breaking glass. Opening the living room door into the hallway, they were confronted with a shattered light bulb on the floor. Thinking this had fallen from the light fitting above them, they looked up, but were surprised to find that the bulb was still intact.

They headed upstairs to check the lights there and discovered that the bulb had come out of a small box room at the head of the stairs. What was particularly strange was that if the bulb had just fallen out, it would have landed on the carpet in the room, and it seemed impossible for it to have landed at the bottom of the stairs. They soon began to realise that this wasn't a natural occurrence, as it began to happen on a regular basis.

Further light bulbs were found in the same place at the foot of the stairs, but were now missing from other rooms of the house. As these occurrences began to intensify, they were accompanied by piano music, but the source of the music could never be identified. Even if traced to the room from where it seemed to be emitting, as soon as they opened the door, the music would stop.

More worrying for the couple, the activity increased even more when powercuts started to plunge the house into complete darkness on a weekly basis. This was odd because none of their neighbours suffered the same powercuts. They contacted the electricity company and had all the wiring in the property checked several times, but investigations revealed that there were no faults to the wiring system.

The most frightening experience occurred during one of these powercuts. The young lady was in the house alone one night and went to the kitchen for a drink. As she stood at the kitchen sink the lights flickered and went out, and the piano music began to play. Turning around to locate a torch, she was met by a young man, leaning against the door with his arms folded, he seemed to have appeared from nowhere. He was dark-haired, and wore an old white dress shirt and trousers, and was smiling at her with a leering gesture. She screamed hysterically and the apparition disappeared.

Fearing for her safety, the couple soon moved out of the property, and are unaware if the activity continues today.

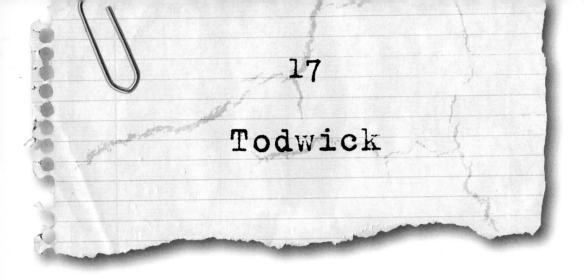

17

Todwick

The Todwick Highwayman

Todwick is a quaint village sporting many fine old farm buildings. However, all is not as it seems.

At Christmas time in the late 1980s, a local woman was driving home from a party that she had been to in Sheffield. Even though it was late, she wasn't tired, and had not consumed any alcohol due to the fact that she had to drive home.

It was just before midnight as she arrived at the notorious accident black spot of Todwick crossroads, next to the Red Lion hotel. She was about to turn right when a dark shape appeared directly in front of her car, illuminated by the headlights. She described this as a man sitting on a black stallion, wearing a long, black, flowing cape which was spread out over the horse. He sported a three-cornered hat, similar to that of an old tricorn type. The horse and rider had galloped out in front of her car and disappeared over a hedge. The woman had heard the legend of this ghost and was more surprised than frightened at her late-night encounter.

Other motorists have also reported seeing the dark figure on horseback, but again have been more surprised than frightened at the site of this once-dangerous villain, who would have robbed unsuspecting travellers at pistol point.

Todwick crossroads.
(Authors' collection)

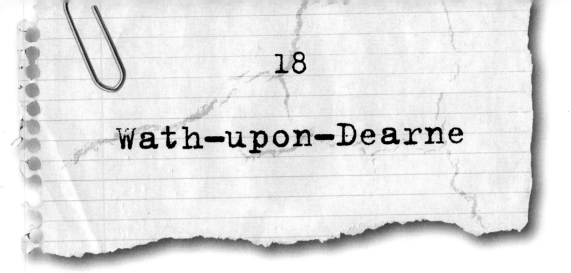

18

Wath-upon-Dearne

Dearne Valley Printers

Dearne Valley Printers is based in a former eighteenth-century public house named the Nelson Inn. It is to be found just off Doncaster Road at Wath, next to an industrial estate. The building has survived decades of regeneration and previously stood proudly amongst rows of pre-war terraces, until their demolition in the 1970s. Some people may perhaps remember the area for the terrible smell that was emitted from Manvers Coking Plant, located at the rear. Locals would often hold their breath whilst travelling past on the bus because the smell was so bad.

During the month of August 2005, renovations were being carried out to the building, after the owners of the printers decided that alteration and improvements were needed for their business. Not wanting to close the company down whilst these works were untaken, contractors were asked to do the renovations out of office hours to prevent disruption to the printers' working day.

Paul Collins and his colleague Dave were drafted in to do the last fixings, which included plastering, hanging doors and renewing light and socket fittings, and were allocated five days in which to complete the work.

Day One

On the first night they arrived at the property, Paul remembers that it was really hot and humid because he was having difficulties with the drying times of the plaster, and it wasn't long before he began to work up a sweat. After making good progress throughout the night, they were disrupted by a sudden drop in temperature, to the point they had goosebumps and could clearly see each other's breath.

Dearne Valley Printers, formerly the Nelson Inn. (Authors' collection)

This was strange due to the temperature being over 30°C during the day and not dropping too much at night. Looking at the clock, Paul remembered noticing that it was dead on 3 a.m. As they were discussing the strange temperature drop and what could have caused it, they were silenced by the distinct sound of footsteps coming from above. Paul said it sounded like hob-nailed boots, or maybe expensive stiletto shoes tapping across the bare wooden floors of the corridors upstairs. Stunned, they both stood looking at the ceiling in disbelief, trying to rationalise what the noise could be.

Convinced that there was an intruder in the building, Paul ran upstairs to confront the mystery person, while Dave waited downstairs to block their escape route. Paul was mystified to discover that all the doors running off corridor were locked, and that no one was in any of the offices. Trying to dismiss what they had heard, they carried on with their work without further disturbance.

Day Two
Paul and Dave started work as usual, but this time on opposite sides of the room – a good twenty-five metres apart. When again the temperature dropped, Paul shouted to Dave, 'It's gone right cold again, can tha feel it?'

Dave shouted back, 'I was just about to say same.' Looking at his watch, he said, 'It's three o'clock – the same as last night.' They continued with their work, when Dave suddenly leaped up into the air and screamed, 'Gerroff me Paul ya bastard. I supposed you think that's funny!' Paul, who was still working on the other side of the room, shouted, 'What's up?' but Dave had fled the building.

Following him outside, Paul discovered Dave sitting down, quite clearly shaken by something. Dave explained that he had felt someone grab hold of him from behind. At first he thought it was Paul trying to scare

him, but, upon turning around, there was no one there.

He told Paul that he was going home and wasn't going to work there anymore. However, Paul calmed him down and told him to go to the twenty-four-hour supermarket to get some food and drink so he could pull himself together. He returned about half an hour later and decided that he would carry on working, but would hurry the job along, so they didn't have to stay there a moment longer than they had to.

Day Three
Still shaken from the previous night, Dave and Paul stayed pretty close together whilst working, in case anything should happen. Three o'clock came around and again the room temperature began to drop. Warily they stopped work and waited with baited breath at to what the next instalment would be. Suddenly, both Paul and Dave saw a figure in a long coat, with the lapels turned up to cover the face, at the far end of the room in which they were working. Paul said it was hard to distinguish if it was male or female, and at first thought the figure was a shadow reflecting in from the window. However, after looking closer at it, they could see that in fact it was freestanding and was inside the building with them. Far from being shy, it seemed to want to make itself known to them by pacing up and down. This went on for several minutes, so Paul got up to take a closer look, but the figure disappeared. This was shortly followed by the distinct sound of printing plates being rattled violently in one of the rooms upstairs, after which they were left undisturbed to finish their work.

They decided to wait around the following morning for one of the printers to arrive and ask if they could explain what they had witnessed over the past few nights. The manager was the first to arrive, so Paul asked him outright if the printing works were haunted. In reply, the manager just smiled knowingly and went about his business.

Day Four

Arriving on site, the pair decided that enough was enough and this was going to be the last night they worked there. They planned to pull out all the stops and complete the job by morning. As 3 a.m. approached, the pair waited to see what the night was going to bring them this time. All of a sudden, as Paul describes it, 'All hell let loose'. All the lights in the building came on, all the computers turned on, all the printers started up and the phones began ringing simultaneously. Both men retreated outside and watched as the chaos unfolded in the unmanned building. Paul explained that lights were flashing on and off in the different rooms of the building and the noise from the phones and printers could be heard clearly outside. Knowing that they couldn't stay outside all night, Paul went back in and answered the phone, thinking it could be a security check call, but on picking up the phone he said that it was a silent phone call, the ones where you know someone is there but they aren't speaking. So he hung up the phone, only for it to start ringing again around a minute later. Again he picked it up only to hear a deathly silence from the caller. Again he hung up and decided to try and turn all the power off in the building to silence the machines and turn out the lights, when the phone started to ring again. This time he decided not to answer it and to concentrate on shutting down the machines. He was stopped in his tracks by the screech of a woman shouting 'pick it up', so he lifted the handset and discovered that there was now a dialling tone, at the same time all the lights and power went off, leaving him in silence and darkness once more.

Dave refused to enter the building again and waited outside whilst Paul finished the last of the work and retrieved their tools.

Several months later

Paul later met up with Joe and explained to him what had happened whilst Dave and he were there. Joe asked Paul if he could arrange for us to investigate the building to see if we could find the answers to what they had experienced on those four nights in August. Paul contacted the printers, who agreed we could go in and conduct the investigation some time in the New Year.

However, our investigation was cancelled due to the arrest of the manager in connection with a longstanding rape case spanning some twenty years, known now as the 'Shoe Rapist'. What seems strange from all of this is that police later found more than 100 pairs of stiletto shoes hidden behind a trapdoor at the printing works.

Paul now seems to think that this may have had some connection to what he and Dave experienced whilst working there. But I guess we'll never know.

Newhill Park Mausoleum

The Mausoleum in Newhill Park, Wath, is known locally as the vault, and records show that it holds the bodies of the Payne family, who owned Newhill Hall, which stood where Newhill Park is today. The Payne family had lived at the Hall since it was built in 1785 by Richard Payne, who was a well-known breeder of polo ponies, and was said to be one of the best sportsmen in the country and won numerous prizes at shows for his horses and ponies. However, his state of mind was questionable; one story has him galloping through the house on one of his prized ponies, damaging furniture as he went. This rumour echoed through the village at the time and people often questioned his sanity.

After the last of the Payne family died, in about 1920, squatters moved into the house and trashed the place. It is said that Richard Payne was so angry that his beautiful home was ruined, he mounted his favourite stallion and rode from the crypt into the hall to frighten the squatters away, as he once had been reported doing many years ago. Locals say that sometimes, late at night, they can hear strange noises coming from the vault, and occasionally the sound of Payne on his horse, galloping to where the building once stood.

One man known to us, who wishes to remain anonymous, was returning home one evening late from the pub, when he decided to relieve himself against the vault. Leaning his arm against the stone monument to steady himself, he heard the distinct sound of a horse rearing and a rider's whip crack. At this point he lost his balance before falling over the wall onto Cemetery Road. Returning home bloodied form his fall, he recounted the incident to his bemused wife, who to this day doesn't believe his story, even though he insists the encounter was real.

Wath Wood Hospital

Wathwood Hospital is now a sixty-bed medium-secure unit. Located in an area of natural beauty, comprising of open countryside and mature woodland, it caters for those individuals who require assessment and treatment for mental health in a secure environment.

During the time when it was a general hospital, staff and patients reported seeing the ghost of a Roman soldier. Nurses said that he would only appear at night, after they had received a new admission into the ward, and that he only ever seemed to inspect the patient as they slept.

We have always been intrigued by ghosts that reputedly haunt hospitals. With tens of thousands of people dying in wards across the UK each year, one could easily come to the logical conclusion that hospitals are replete with restless souls manifesting, demanding justice or just not understanding their predicament.

The mausoleum at Newhill Park. (Authors' collection)

Wathwood Hospital today.
(Authors' collection)

An old photograph of Wath
Gaol. (Authors' collection)

Wath Gaol

Like most small towns, Wath is steeped in history, and not many people are aware that it holds its very own gaol, which was formerly used as a debtor's prison. However, this is in private ownership now and has been turned into a residential property.

Originally, the building incorporated two cells, which both included small pierced holes to allow light in, along with separate toilets to each cell. Above these rooms was the main constables' room, which housed a small fireplace.

Prior to the house being turned into a residential dwelling, reports were made that an ex-police officer, dressed in an old-fashioned uniform complete with cape, haunted his former station. In addition, whispering voices could be heard in the cells when they were empty.

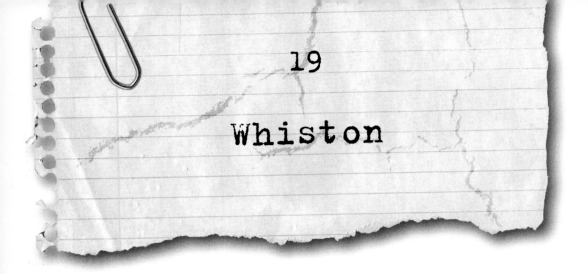

19

Whiston

Ravings of a Late Night Recital

Whiston was once a busy village located at the side of a major road network, said to be one of the greatest highways to the north of England. Many travellers would visit and stay there. Today, Whiston is a quiet Rotherham village, rather more off the beaten track than it would once have been.

Back in 1947, an up-and-coming musician became a regular visitor to the church at Whiston, due to it being the only place where a suitable pipe organ was situated at the time. So frequent was his visits to the church, the vicar gave him a key to the building so that he could practise during the evening, when services were not in progress.

One winter's night, he unlocked the church as normal and began to practise alone. The church was in darkness apart from the lantern light flickering over the organ itself. Suddenly he heard the sound of hurried footsteps moving down the isle of the church on the stone floor towards him. Turning around to see who it was, he discovered that there was no one there. Curious, he stood up from his organ stool to investigate the footsteps, think-

ing it was someone playing tricks on him. He heard the door latch to the vestry click as it opened and closed. This was used to house the choristers' garments and other materials. Although he couldn't see anything, he followed the mysterious sounds and entered the room, which was in complete darkness.

Calling out to the person who he thought had entered, he was relieved when he received no reply, but suddenly he became aware of a strange chill enveloping him, followed by what he described as a gruff wheezing and groaning sound breathing down his neck. Petrified at this encounter, he dared not take a breath himself for what seemed like eternity, until he finally mustered up enough courage to flee the church and swore never to practise there alone again!

Repeatedly telling his story to other frequenters of the church, he came across tales from many others who had heard the same footsteps and experienced the chilled atmosphere. However, they always seem to offer the same rational explanations, stating that the church was old and it could indeed be creaking pews or old heating pipes.

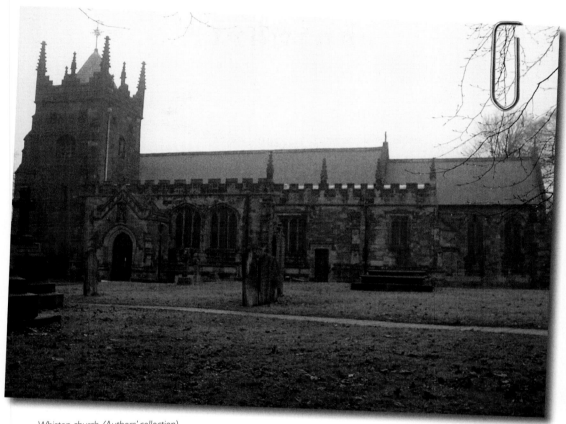

Whiston church. (Authors' collection)

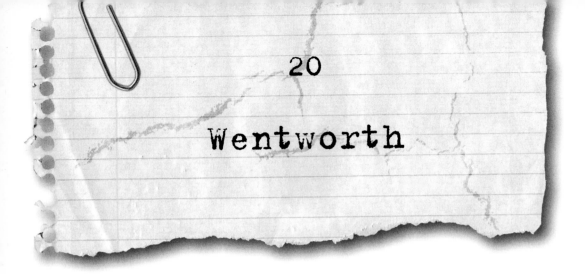

20

Wentworth

WENTWORTH has to be our favourite place in South Yorkshire, due the amount of paranormal activity here, ranging from the unusual to the outright frightening. Each of the old buildings seem to have a story to tell. We lovingly call it the mini York, and we are quite lucky to live close to this historically packed location. In this section we have collated some of our favourite stories from the area.

The history of Wentworth is inextricably linked with the history of the great aristocratic families – the Wentworths, Watsons and Fitzwilliams – who presided over the village for centuries, until recently, following the end of the Fitzwilliam family bloodline in 1979, when a trust was founded to enable the legacy of the Wentworth estate to remain intact.

Wentworth Woodhouse

We'll start with the most famous part of Wentworth, Wentworth Woodhouse. The East Front of the house is visible from Wentworth Park and is a magnificent structure over 600 feet in length. It is famous as the longest frontage of any country house in England and consists of 365 rooms. Unfortunately, this is all the public can see of the house, as it is now privately owned. However, for those walking past who want to know a bit more about the history of the place here is a brief history of the building and its owners throughout the years.

Wentworth Woodhouse.
(Courtesy of Rotherhamweb)

The Wentworths

The village dates back to at least 1066, when lands in the area were a tribute to Adam de Newmarch and William le Flemming, later passing to the canons of Bolton Abbey. To this day it is not known how the Wentworth family came into ownership, but around 1300 they married into the Woodhouse family, who lived outside the village, on the site of what is now Wentworth Woodhouse.

The Watsons

The 2nd Earl of Strafford inherited his father's title, but died without an heir and subsequently passed the estate on to the Watson family. It was the Watson-Wentworth's who built most of the grand structures in the area, including the magnificent East Front of Wentworth Woodhouse and the follies of Hoober Stand and Keppel's Column. Unfortunately, he didn't find time to produce an heir and so the estate changed hands once again to the Fitzwilliams

The Fitzwilliams

The Fitzwilliams took the estate over in 1782 and were responsible for much of the early industrial development in the area, establishing numerous mines and factories in the surrounding towns and villages. This made the family even wealthier, and by the mid-nineteenth century they were the sixth wealthiest landowners in the country.

The Fitzwilliam family reign continued until the death of the 10th earl in 1979, leaving the estate in the hands of a trust, which continues to preserve the character of the village. However, Wentworth Woodhouse is now under private ownership, and little is known about future plans for the grand structure.

The Exterior of the Building

Wentworth Woodhouse is actually two houses, both largely rebuilt in the eighteenth century. The East Front, which we see from the park, entirely obscures the second house, which faces west towards the village. Thomas Watson-Wentworth, who built most of the house we see today, evidently became dissatisfied with the West Front whilst it was being built, so he commissioned further work to be carried out on the East Front around 1734.

The Interior of the Building

The main entrance to the house is via the Pillared Hall, accessed from the east entrance. This gives access to some of the ground floor rooms and, via a grand staircase, to the Marble Saloon, a 60 foot square room some 40 feet high, which is the main reception room in the house.

South of here are two grand rooms named after the paintings that once hung in them, the Van Dyke Room and the Whistlejacket Room. To the north of the Marble Saloon lies another huge room, the Long Gallery. This is 130 feet long and again once contained an exquisite collection of paintings and other artworks.

The First Earl of Strafford Sighting

The most famous Wentworth family member was Thomas Wentworth, 1st Earl of Strafford, who entered Parliament and progressed rapidly through the ranks, becoming Lord President of the Council of the North and Lord Lieutenant of Ireland.

Thomas Wentworth resided in Wentworth Woodhouse at the time of King Charles I, acting as administrator to the royal family, until he was beheaded in 1641 for political treachery.

His head was impaled on a spike at the Tower of London as a warning to others, but close friends secretly smuggled his body back to the hall-house in Hooton Roberts, now known as the Earl of Strafford public house. This was formerly one of the principal seats of the earl. He was secretly buried in the church next to the property. Legend has it that the house has a series of secret tunnels leading to the church and nearby Conisbrough Castle. These very tunnels are said to have transported Thomas during the dead of night.

After his death, his widow lived in the house by the church until her burial by torch-light in the chancel in 1688. Locals could never understand why, when she had such a grand house back in Wentworth. It had always been thought that her husband was buried at Holy Trinity Church, Wentworth, where there is a memorial to him, but in 1895, when renovations at St John's Church in Hooton Roberts were carried out, a horrific discovery was made. Three skeletons were found lying together, one with no skull, one belonging to an old lady, and one a deformed child. Local legend has it that these skeletons are the remains of Thomas, his wife Margaret and their child.

His ghost is believed to appear at 11 p.m. each night, walking down the stairs from the oldest part of Wentworth Woodhouse, roam-ing down the old oak-panelled corridors where his living accommodation was once situated. Additional reports have been made that at certain times of the year he is seen walking down Haigh Lane from Wentworth house carrying his head under his arm. His tragic death clearly affected his spirit.

Just before the First World War, a cleaner at the manor came face-to-face with the ghost of Thomas Wentworth; his spectre appeared on the stone staircase across the courtyard, inside the north wing. It was late one night and after lighting the gas lamp at the foot of the stairs she ascended the short flight, and began scrubbing the top step. For some reason she lost her grip on the scrubbing brush and it clattered to the bottom of the stairs and, grudgingly, she descended after her cleaning tool. After she had stooped to pick up the brush she turned around and saw on the wall the shadow of a man. She looked towards the source of the dark shape cast before her and was shocked to see the figure of 'a grey gen-tleman in Stuart dress', standing at the top of the stairs. A chilling breeze suddenly whipped up around her as the ghost began his descent towards her. She stood transfixed, taking little notice of the gaslight behind her, as it danced with the fresh current of air. The ghost com-pleted his descent of the stairway and passed through her without a trace of hesitation.

The cleaner, shocked at this, said she had recognised the man from a painting hung in

St John's Church, Hooton Roberts, where the Earl of Strafford was secretly buried. (Authors' collection)

the great house and that she knew who he was straight away. She continued to work there for many years, but never saw his apparition again.

Years later, a caretaker gave a very accurate description of the same phantom, right down to the britches. The man in question encountered Wentworth's spirit above the same stairs in the old gallery. For some reason an oil painting had fallen from the wall and as the caretaker bent down to pick the portrait up, he saw the same apparition walk across the room towards him. Again, the encounter caused the victim to freeze in petrifaction and this time, instead of passing through the shocked witness, Wentworth merely came to a halt in front of the employee and regarded him ominously. The caretaker quickly recovered from the shock and dashed out of the building, vowing never to return and forever remaining intransigent on the subject.

To this day, people have claimed to feel the same cold breeze, and have sensed the presence of someone behind them, and have reported to have even run out of the building screaming hysterically. Despite the history of the house, many people who have resided there have described its atmosphere as 'friendly' and 'lived-in', despite the fact that Thomas Wentworth's ghost is expected to appear at its usual time of 11 o' clock!

The Phantom Lady of Wentworth House

The identity of this spectre is not known, although is speculated to be one of two possible ladies. Many believe it to be Lady Mary Bright, wife of Charles Wentworth, and only daughter of Colonel Stephen Bright of nearby Carbrook Hall. The second suggestion is that of a disgraced member of the Fitzwilliam dynasty, who brought shame on the family with her lust-driven encounters with one of the footman, and who continues to sneak through the darkened corridors to continue her illicit affair.

After the house became a college, students reported feeling as though they were 'being watched' and several even felt the sensation of being 'prevented' from climbing the stairs by an invisible force.

The Phantom Monk of Wentworth House

Again there are two trains of thought regarding the appearance of this long-dead monk. One is that the original site of Wentworth Woodhouse's West Front was acquired somewhat controversially upon the Dissolution of Bolton Abbey, and that one of its brethren still walks in search of his monastic connections. The second suggestion relates to the controversial purchase by Thomas Wentworth of pillars and stone from Monk Bretton Priory (for the princely sum of £700) to use in the building of a new aisle in the old church at Wentworth – to house the monuments of his father and himself. If the latter is the case, then many believe that this mysterious apparition could be the victim of a residual haunting, with the monk having strong emotional ties to his former monastery.

In addition to this, it is alleged that there are tunnels leading from the mansion through to Monk Bretton Priory in Barnsley, Hooton Roberts and Roche Abbey at Maltby, where the monks sought refuge during the Dissolution of the Monasteries by Henry VIII. There are said to be entrances to eight tunnels – arranged like the spokes on a wheel – at Welbeck Abbey, the Duke of Portland's land. According to hearsay around Rotherham, there are tunnels under the town centre and up to Wentworth House and also Hellaby Hall.

The Stable Block Haunting

The stable block was built in 1768 by John Carr on a scale to match the house. This can easily be viewed from the public footpath that runs through Wentworth Park. The stables comprise of fifteen bays with a rusticated entrance with Tuscan columns, pediment and cupola. There is a large fountain in the centre of the courtyard, which can be seen through the main gates.

The Wentworth Woodhouse estate has always been an extensive and profitable area. In its heyday, child labour was prevalent. It is well documented that the peasant children of Wentworth lived in extremely harsh conditions and fatal illness and tragic accidents were quite common. Such was the plight of the children that Lady Mabel Smith, formerly of the Wentworth Woodhouse dynasty, went to great lengths to try to improve their welfare.

There is a tragic tale, although not much is documented, of a child who was cut down in his youth while going about his daily toils. After extensive research we found that the following story does seem to have some truth in it, though this particular aspect of Wentworth's history remains open to speculation and is tinged with countless accounts of local folkloric records.

The 2nd marquis' favourite horse, Whistejacket, was housed in the stables. The stable master had come to the stable block one day and saw that the stable door had been left open. Furious at this, he scolded the young stable boy, who was in charge of its upkeep, by beating him with his crop. The boy ran to close the stable door, but didn't see the horse and cart travelling through the grand archway of the block and was trampled to death.

Since then, reported sightings of the boy have been witnessed by many visitors to the area, particularly when the grounds were used as a college up until the early 1980s. It is claimed that a young boy can be seen running across the courtyard and the sound of horse's hooves and his disembodied screams can be heard echoing around the square.

The Rockingham Mausoleum

The Rockingham Mausoleum was built in 1788 by William, 1st Earl Fitzwilliam, as a memorial to his uncle, Charles, 2nd Marquis of Rockingham (1730-82). The monument stands in a secluded, private wood and is open to the public between 2 p.m. and 5 p.m. on Sunday between spring and the August bank holiday. Unlike the other Wentworth follies, it may not be viewed, even from the outside, except at these times or with special permission from:

Fitzwilliam Wentworth Amenity Trust,
Clayfield Lane, Wentworth
Rotherham, South Yorkshire S62 7TD

Wentworth House Stable Block.
(Authors' collection)

The lowest section is externally square with a door on the west side and windows on the other three sides. The inside is a circular room with a domed ceiling, supported by columns and containing four niches in which are displayed statues of eight of the marquis's close friends, these include Admiral Keppel, for whom Rockingham built Keppel's Column. Inside is the life-sized statue of the marquis, expertly carved in white marble by the infamous British sculptor of the time, Joseph Nollekens, for the princely sum of £3,000 – then an audacious amount of money.

The mausoleum is a magnificent structure, 90 feet high and standing on a large base surrounded by four obelisks, each over half the height of the mausoleum. It is protected by a high iron fence running around the perimeter of the base, and has a gate on the west side before the mausoleum's door.

Designed by John Carr, a York architect, the work took just three years and was carried out by ten men. The building has three tiers, each with a distinctive style. The topmost section of the mausoleum is designed in the style of a Roman temple and consists of a cupola supported by twelve columns. Large urns stand at the four corners.

The middle section consists of four open arches covering the sarcophagus, which is open to the elements. The sarcophagus itself is only decorative and the remains of the marquis are interred in the Strafford family vault in York Minster. The top of this section bears the carved inscription:

> This monument was erected by William, Earl Fitzwilliam, 1788.
> To the memory of Charles, Marquis of Rockingham.

The marble statue of Charles, 2nd Marquis of Rockingham by Nollekens, situated inside the mausoleum. (Authors' collection)

Although Nollekens actually lived to the ripe old age of eighty-five, a strange legend evolved that he committed suicide when it was pointed out to him that he had forgotten some of the stitching on the left foot of the marquis's statue. However unlikely, he was renowned for his attention to detail, and once this discrepancy was pointed out to him, and due to his age could never rectify his mistake, he took his own life.

Prior to the site being renovated in the year 2000, and while it was derelict, it was said to be used for black masses. The Black Mass is a ceremony and inversion, or parody, of the Catholic mass, that was indulged in apparently for the purpose of mocking Christianity and worshipping Satan; a rite that was said to traditionally involve human sacrifice as well as obscenity and blasphemy of horrific proportions. However, no evidence of this was ever found there, apart from signs of black candle wax, and animal remains.

Hoober Stand that can be seen from miles around. (Authors' collection)

Once the restoration had taken place and security was increased, these alleged activities ceased. However, since then, evidence of this type of activity have been found at Hoober Stand.

The History of Hoober Stand

The Stand itself was built in 1747-8 to commemorate defeat of the Jacobite Rebellion in 1745, when the 1st Marquis (then plain Thomas Watson Wentworth) fought on the side of King George II. In recognition of his contribution, the king elevated Wentworth to marquis, and the new marquis decided to build the 30-meter tower to show his gratitude.

The folly is a three-sided pyramid, in Ionic style. Each of its three sides is 42 feet wide at ground level and begins with a slightly tapering base over twice the height of a man. From the top of the base, the walls narrow at a greater angle to end at an iron-railed platform, 24 feet wide on each side, about 85 feet from the ground. Entrance is by way of a door on the southern wall, with an inscription above the doorway which reads:

> This pyramidal building was erected by his Majesty's most dutiful subject Thomas Marquess of Rockingham in grateful respect to the preserver of our religious laws and liberty's King George the Second who, by the blessing of God having subdued a most unnatural rebellion in Britain anno 1746 maintains the balance of power and settles a just and honorable peace in Europe 1748.

From the doorway leads a spiral staircase of 155 steps. Winding to the left, they ascend to the viewing platform. The staircase is lighted by five recessed windows, each provided with a seat for the weary. It finally emerges under an octagonal domed cupola, some 15 feet in height, which brings the total height of Hoober Stand to a little less than 100 feet. From the platform, on a clear day, it is possible to see York Minster some forty miles distant.

The Caves of Hoober Stand

In close proximity to Hoober Stand lies a labyrinth of caves and tunnels, which unfortunately have been sealed up to prevent access. Archaeologists suggest that these may have once been burial chambers, although the debate continues as to their proper constitution. Nevertheless, there are reports of strange phenomena occurring around the entrances to this day, including a ghostly apparition and supposed witchcraft being practiced.

People have reported witnessing folk dancing naked around camp fires from afar, raising suspicions that magical rites of passage take place there. Evidence has been found in the form of sacrificial offerings and occult symbols, normally that of pentagrams, and mutilated remains of birds and small mammals, this gives credence to the stories mentioned earlier relating to the mausoleum.

An apparition appears outside the cave entrance in the form of a man dressed in druid sacrificial robes, and is aggressive towards anyone who dare venture close to the opening. It then walks straight through the reinforced steel that barricades the entrance and disappears into the bowels of the cave.

Unlike a normal residential haunting, he is thought to be that of an elemental entity, summoned by the occult activity that takes place there, though not considered to have any direct links to the monument in any way.

Our Findings at Hoober Stand

Richard read a report on the internet one evening about paranormal activities taking place at Hoober Stand, including tales of

The inscription above the doorway. (Authors' collection)

The cave entrance is now sealed off. (Authors' collection)

Evidence of witchcraft found whilst taking photos for this book. (Authors' collection)

witchcraft, hooded figures and disembodied screams coming from the tower late at night. So, on 6 December 2003, around 11 p.m., Richard armed himself with a digital camera and set off to the folly.

Upon arrival nothing seemed out of the ordinary, it was a dark, cold night and the skies were clear. The moon shone through the trees onto the ground and gave the area a mystical feel. He wasted no time and set about taking photographs randomly of the folly and surrounding area. Before long, he started to get the eerie feeling that he was being observed from a window in the tower, and, quickly snapping his last few photos of the folly, he left the site.

Upon arriving home, he downloaded the pictures he had taken onto his computer, not expecting to see much – perhaps a few orbs/light anomalies, but to his amazement he had captured an image of a figure in the window of the building about halfway up. Richard can confirm that no one was in the building at the time and that no lights were on inside either.

Puzzled by this and the evidence that he seemed to have caught, he decided to go back the following evening at the same time to take more pictures to see if he could debunk

his photographic anomaly. As he suspected, the figure did not reappear.

Prior to Richard and Joe meeting, Joe had been viewing the website in 2004 where Richard published his findings and decided to take a visit to the site, to see if he could find an explanation for the photo. Dragging along a reluctant friend, they arrived at the folly in the dead of night, in mid-February. After wandering around the area and getting their bearings to try and find the same spot that Richard had taken the photo, Joe's friend decided to return to his car after loosing interest, leaving Joe sitting alone on the steps of the grand folly.

Not long after his friend had left him, Joe was startled by a noise coming from the hedgerow. Clambering to his feet, he approached the hedge, only to realise that it was a sheep. His laugh out loud at his own expense was cut short by a loud bang coming from the very doorway he had just been sitting at. Staggering back in shock, he took a deep breath and slowly approached the folly to ascertain what had caused the bang. He neared the doorway, lent forward and pressed his ear against the thick wooden door, only to hear a faint shuffling and footsteps coming from within.

Excited by his findings, he returned to the car to bring his friend to listen to the unexplained noise coming from within. After standing outside the folly for a further ten to fifteen minutes without hearing the noise, a dispute broke out over the credibility of Joe's alleged experience, only to be broken by a disembodied shriek that seemed to ascend the tower. Joe's friend, spooked at what he had just heard, insisted that they leave or Joe could walk home alone. Of course Joe reluctantly agreed – who wants to walk 6 miles?

The photo taken by Richard which, along with some orbs, shows the outline of a figure in an upstairs window. (Authors' collection)

Both Richard and Joe revisited the site on numerous occasions, but have yet to experience anything as dramatic as they had before.

Could the figure seen standing in the upper-floor window of this magnificent folly be that of Charles Wentworth, gazing out over his the extensive estate that he, his father and many of his ancestors had amassed with amazing rapidity in previous years?

Needle's Eye and Vinegar Stone

The Needle's Eye is a 45 foot (14 metre) high, sandstone block pyramid with an ornamental urn on the top and a tall Gothic ogee arch through the middle, which straddles a disused roadway. It was built in 1780, allegedly to win a bet after the 2nd Marquis claimed he could drive a coach and horses through the eye of a needle. This may refer to the biblical saying that it is easier for a camel to go through the eye of a needle than for a rich man to enter the kingdom of God. At this time, Rockingham

was one of the richest men in England. Legend has it that the wager was only a fraction of the cost of the construction price when built; the marquis was an eccentric individual indeed.

The eastern face of the pyramid shows the spread pattern of musket ball impact holes, undoubtedly caused by a volley of musket fire, which looks to have been fired from no more than ten yards. The pattern clearly indicates a target at the height of a man's heart, possibly of two individuals.

Dog walkers around November frequently report seeing a mist emitting from the eastern face of the folly, some saying that it forms the shape of the unlucky men. What is particularly strange is the distinctive smell of gunpowder in the area, as though the shootings had just taken place.

Surrounding the evidence of execution, mould and lichen grow in the shape of two slumped bodies. If you cannot see them, try squinting at the foot of the folly and all should become clear. The reason for the discoloration is obvious; shrubbery growing against the pyramid has recently been cleared. The question remains: Why was it only growing over the musket ball pits?

Clockwise from above:

The vinegar stone, complete with offering. (Authors' collection)

The junction of Coaley Lane where the old woman is seen. (Authors' collection)

Musket spread on the wall of the folly. (Authors' collection)

Not too far away from the folly, as you leave the footpath on to Coaley Lane, is an old stone dish about a foot square and covered in moss. This was used as a vinegar stone during the plague; people would deposit coins in the vinegar and take goods left at the stone to prevent the spreading of the disease.

The ghostly apparition of an old lady is seen crossing over the road from Street Lane to the site of the vinegar stone. She's described as a crooked old hag, stooped over and carrying a sack over her shoulder. Motorists have witnessed the apparition appear in their headlights, forcing them to brake hard, only for her to continue across the road, oblivious of the danger, and stoop over to inspect the vinegar stone as if she is searching for coins that people have left.

Legend has it that if you leave a coin at the vinegar stone and make a wish, the old hag will reward your kindness.

Keppel's Column

At 115 feet, Keppel's Column is the tallest of the Wentworth follies; it was originally planned to be even taller and capped with a statue of Admiral Keppel, but evidently the Marquis of Rockingham ran short of funds. It was designed by John Carr, who was also responsible for the Wentworth Woodhouse stables and the family's Irish house at Coollattin.

Admiral Keppel was a friend of the marquis and a fellow Whig, who was court-martialled following a naval defeat at the hands of the French in 1777. The marquis had already planned to build a pillar to mark the southern boundary of his park, but following Keppel's acquittal he adapted the design and aimed to create a triumphant pillar by way of celebrating what he saw as a defeat for the government.

The tower, which has an internal spiral staircase, was open to the public until the 1960s, but it is now in a dangerous condition and is kept locked. The current owner is Rotherham Borough Council. It isn't known if there are any plans to reopen the tower, but now that the other Wentworth follies are all open at various times, it's a shame it's not possible to take in the complete set! In the meanwhile you can view the tower at close quarters from the public footpath running from Admiral's Crest in Scholes.

Ghostly sightings have been reported at the tower over generations right up until the present day, of a woman ascending the staircase by candlelight in a state of distress, and can be heard wailing from a distance away.

The unknown female is rumoured to be a member of the Rockinghams, who allegedly had an affair with a married family friend to the disgrace of her relatives. While using the excuse of going riding, she would meet with him at the remote location for their secret jaunts. When the family honour was threatened, he callously broke off the liaison at their last meeting.

After her death, from a broken heart, she continued to appear at Keppel's Column, where she once would meet her lover to engage in secret trysts.

One of the more recent sightings of the mysterious wailing woman was in the 1990s, when a local girl, who grew up around the area, was walking home at around eleven o'clock one evening. Conscious of the time, she took a shortcut home through the woods which came out at the folly. She heard the sound of a woman crying, coming from the direction of the gloomy building. Peering through the darkness to try and locate where the sound was coming from, and thinking that someone may be in trouble, she approached the gothic structure slowly, her heart pounding, and could clearly hear the sound of crying coming from within. This bewildered her, for she knew that the building had been closed for many years. She looked all round and couldn't see anything, but then noticed a light at the bottom window of the tower. Confused, she watched it go up to the next window, and could still hear the disturbing cries. At that point terror gripped her and she ran home as fast as she could, only to be scolded by her mother for her lateness, even though she tried to explain to her what she had witnessed.

To this day, the young woman still gets spooked by what she saw and heard on that frightful night.

Keppel's Column, where the wailing woman has been heard. (Authors' collection)

The Bear Pit and Wentworth Gardens

The Bear Pit is accessible by the garden centre and built on two levels with a spiral staircase.

Watson and Pritchett designed it in the early 1800s. Set beneath an overgrown earth mound is a grotto-style entrance, guarded by two life-sized statues of Roman soldiers. A curved tunnel leads to two vaulted cells, internal steps rise to a landing and upper entrance doorway in a Jacobean style, with extravagantly-carved ornamental piers which house a cast-iron plaque over the upper doorway, which reads:

> There is a healing in the garden
> When one longs for peace and pardon
> Once past the gate no need to wait
> For God is in the garden.

This Bear Pit was once the home of a bear, whose keeper lived in one of the nearby cottages. Sadly, the Jacobean doorway was removed from Wentworth Woodhouse in about 1630, before being resituated at the entrance to the Bear Pit in Wentworth Gardens, where it stands today. Obviously the pit is now empty, but it is possible to climb inside and down some steep steps, which lead to the Japanese Garden below.

Sightings of Victorian-era figures have been seen in the gardens, including the apparition of a man dressed like a Victorian pallbearer.

An employee at the garden centre, who was shooting vermin early one evening, saw a man he first thought was a customer, until he notice his strange attire a – like a funeral bearer from the Victorian era. When challenged, the figure vanished into thin air, leaving the worker disbelieving what he had just seen.

Adding credibility to this sighting, a family visiting the gardens recounted a strange experience. Their little boy kept telling his mother he could see a man in old clothes, but she couldn't see anyone and dismissed his claims as that of an overactive imagination.

Weeks later, after developing the photographs of their day out, she was unnerved to see that standing by her son, near the Jacobean entrance, was what appeared to be a tall man wearing a top hat.

Due to child protection laws, we were unable to print this picture.

Other Stories relating to Wentworth

The George and Dragon

The George and Dragon public house is situated on the Main Street in Wentworth. It been licensed since 1804, and remains a free house to this day.

The seventeenth-century former manor house has had many things go bump in the night, including ghostly footsteps coming from the beer cellar, a clock chiming in a sealed-up room, a woman in Victorian dress, and objects thrown across the pub.

The most famous ghost at the George and Dragon is known as the White Lady, and it is believed that she lived here during the nineteenth century. Her spirit is reported to have been seen in the ladies toilet, which is situated in the bar area, and she is described as emerging and disappearing into the wall after frightening the female patrons. She is also blamed for throwing glasses across the bar at unsuspecting bar staff. Little is known of the origins of the White Lady, but it's strongly suspected that she had links to the pub and possibly ran the establishment at some point. Her reason for the haunting is unknown, but we suspect she doesn't like the thought of anyone else encroaching on her domain.

Beneath the bar is the beer cellar, which is accessed by a number of stone steps. Whilst changing barrels, staff have reported feeling a sense of dread, hearing heavy footsteps and smelling a foul stench. Most of the staff won't go down there alone. The spirit is said to be that of an unknown man, and it is his ghost that paranormal investigators have picked up on the most. Psychics and mediums usually describe the apparition as having a knife in his hand.

Outside the building is situated the old barn, which is currently used for private functions, but the upstairs is very rarely used; this is where the sealed attic room is located. Many people have reported hearing the sounds of a clock chiming and hushed conversations coming from within, as well as footsteps walking across the wooden floors.

We have been unable to clarify any of the alleged hauntings in the former manor house, but the idea of a haunted pub in this historical village adds to its charm in our opinion.

The Wentworth Padfoot

There have been many sightings over recent years of a large, black dog-like creature that manifests in the woods and secluded back roads of Wentworth. Witnesses have described it as being as large as a calf, having long black shaggy fur and red eyes (see Aston Stones, p. 52).

The story goes that in the late 1960s, a keen racing cyclist from Wentworth cycled fifty miles every day with a group of friends. One particularly cold and foggy February night, he had finished his training and left his friends to make the journey home. He began to cycle along the lanes at a good pace, hurrying since he did not want to be out any longer than necessary. He had reached a dark, unlit lane between Greasbrough and Wentworth, when he looked to the left of his bicycle and saw a large black dog, similar to a Rottweiler in stature but the size of a Great Dane, running along beside him.

Despite the cold there was no sign of the animal's breath in the air, even though his own was clearly visible. Neither was there any sound of panting; in fact the only sound seemed to be the dog's feet, which splashed as though it was running through water.

The cyclist could feel the hairs on his neck rise, and put on an enormous spurt of speed to outrun the animal. The gradient of the hill was quite steep at this point, but as a racing cyclist, he had no problem picking up speed. He was horrified, however, to look across at the dog and notice that, although it did not even appear to have lengthened its stride, it was still keeping up with him, and its eyes were blood red. The beast kept pace for a further 200 yards, despite the cyclist's strenuous efforts to outrun it, until it ran across his path and into the front wheel. He braced himself for impact, only for it to dematerialise into a waft of black, sooty smoke. Even today, when the man is driving along this route towards Greasbrough, it causes a familiar cold shiver to run down his spine.

Locals at the Rockingham Arms have often overheard unknowing travellers reporting their encounters of the phantom hound along the same stretch of road.

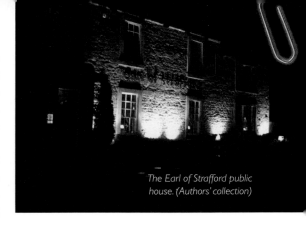

The Earl of Strafford public house. (Authors' collection)

Could this menacing apparition be the spirit of one of the Fitzwilliam hounds, once housed in the world-famous stable and kennel block at Wentworth?

The Earl of Strafford public house, Hooton Roberts

Although the Earl of Strafford isn't in Wentworth, it was originally part of the Wentworth estate.

Once again the authors' paths seem to have crossed prior to them meeting. This story was passed to Richard by a third party, re-accounting Joe's first-hand knowledge of the strange experiences that have occurred there over the years.

The following account was told to Richard. The Kent family took over the estate in the eighteenth century and it's a certain member of this legacy that is still considered to be haunting this public house today. Ann Kent was said to have committed suicide by hanging herself from the banister of the main stairwell. She was angry with her father after he locked her in her room, forbidding her from seeing the local baker's son, who she had fallen madly in love with. Reports have been made that her restless soul is said to still walk the stairs and corridors of this ancient establishment.

However, Joe's account is slightly different, and came from a well-informed source that can't be named in this book and will be

The road where the infamous Wentworth hound appears. (Authors' collection)

referred to as Ms X, this will become apparent later. This version slightly differs in that Ann didn't hang herself from the banister as told to Richard, but in fact was hanged in the dumbwaiter that was situated in her room.

It is not known if this act was intentional or accidental, but it is speculated that she may have being trying to escape from her room, by using the dumb waiter as an elevator, when the cabinet broke and the cord wrapped around her neck, plunging her to her death. It is here that the kitchen staff found Ann's contorted corpse – at the bottom of the dumbwaiter shaft, and not the staircase.

Following the tragedy, the dumbwaiter was removed from the building. Although the location of her death is different, the scenes of her hauntings are the same. The reason that we think Joe's version of events is correct, is that she was locked in her room and wasn't allowed out, thus preventing her from hanging herself from the balcony. This story seems to have been altered over the years, due to the dumbwaiter being removed and the sighting of her ghost seen on the stairs, although numerous reports from staff have been made that cutlery and bizarre accidents have occurred in the kitchen, where the old dumbwaiter once was.

Ms X's Story

Ms X is the main source of Joe's story and has researched the history and reported ghostly sightings at this location over the last thirty years. However, due to the content of the story, she has never revealed her identity.

Thirty years ago, Ms X was a young, naive teenager, and always found the site of the old manor house quite intriguing and frequented the place regularly. One evening she was discussing this place with two male friends, whom she'd recently met at college, and was telling them about the grand, derelict building and stories of the alleged hauntings.

The room where Miss X waited. (Authors' collection)

The lads seemed to take great interest and asked her to show them where it was. It was getting late and Ms X didn't really want to go at that time of night because the place was quite spooky. However, relenting to peer-pressure, she gave in and took them to see it. Upon arriving, they found that the rear of the property was open and realised that they weren't the only people who had been there due to the building being insecure.

They entered the building and started to take a look around. It was then she began to realise that she had been taken there under false pretences, because the lads weren't interested in the ghost stories she had been telling them, but were in fact after the lead from the run-down property.

The boys climbed through the loft hatch and began to strip the lead off the roof. Annoyed at this, she insisted that they leave straight away, but they ignored her pleas and told her that if she wanted a lift home then she would have to wait until they had finished.

Not wanting to be part of the crime, but too scared to walk home alone, she was forced to stay. But refused to be any part of it and walked back down the grand staircase into the room that is now known as the snug, where they had first entered.

Alone, and a little worried at what she had been coerced into, she began to cry in fear that they would be caught. She was soon joined by the youngest lad, who asked if she was OK, while the older one carried on about his crime. Comforting her, he said that everything would be alright as the house was old, it would more than likely be pulled down anyway.

Their conversation was cut short by the toll of the bell striking 1 a.m. from the Church of St John's next door. All of a sudden the temperature fell and the room was plunged into darkness. This was followed by a strange sweeping/dragging sound moving along in time to loud footsteps on the wooden floors above, which seemed to be heading towards the stairwell.

Standing up, their hearts pounding, they edged towards the doorway to the staircase, hoping it was their friend coming down from the roof. What they saw can only be described as an eerie, glowing, florescent blue light, flickering through the banister rails, almost as if a disembodied lantern was being carried down the stairs.

Startled by this, they fled through the open window into the gardens at the rear and began shouting to their friend on the roof, 'Get the hell out of there!' Fearing the police, he ran back through the house, joining them outside. Bemused at their story, he turned to go and collect the lead he'd removed. However, the younger lad and Ms X jumped in the car

and threatened to leave without him, and so he reluctantly joined them.

Years later, after the building was renovated into the Earl of Strafford public house, Ms X was intrigued to read in a local paper about a honeymooning couple staying there, who had been woken up by the ghost of a woman. They described her as being dressed in a long blue gown, with a bustle and flowing petticoats.

A chill ran down Ms X's spine when it dawned on her that this was what she had heard that fateful night – the sound of petticoats and bustle sweeping across the floor in time to the footsteps.

Another one of Ms Xs findings is the story of a waitress, working in the snug one evening. While collecting glasses she thought she saw someone standing outside the window, dressed in Cromwellian-era clothing. She suddenly realised that there wasn't anyone outside, but in fact the reflection of someone standing behind her, inside! Spinning around, there was no one there. Frightened by what she had seen, she left the pub that evening, never to return.

Could this have been another sighting of the Earl of Strafford?

We would like to take this opportunity to thank Ms X … whoever you are.

Conclusion

Although York is regarded as the most haunted city in England, Wentworth may just be the most haunted village,.

The truth behind Wentworth's supernatural events remain shrouded in mystery, and there are many unanswered questions, which can only be unravelled through continuous research and investigation. Fortunately, we reside in the vicinity to remain at the cutting-edge of this crusade.

The staircase, said to be haunted by the ghost of Ann Kent. (Authors' collection)

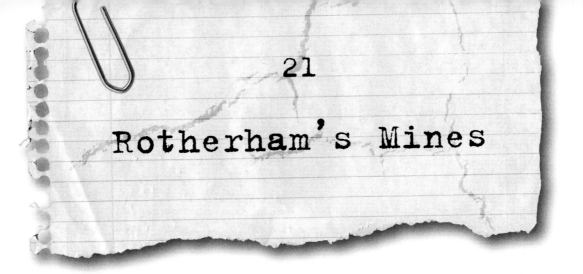

21

Rotherham's Mines

THROUGHOUT the history of mining, death and injury from accidents have been commonplace. In the early days ignorance and lack of safety measures were largely responsible. The miners were often unaware of the dangers or if they were, carried on working regardless, for fear of losing their jobs and their family's being turned out on to the streets. The mine owners cared little for safety, because safety measures meant spending money, hence less profit, and before the unions, the miners had no one to argue their case for them.

Around the turn of the twentieth century, unions were formed and gained large memberships. Public awareness made it necessary for mine owners to take serious action regarding safety. In 1911 an Act of Parliament was passed, which stated that mines must have trained rescue teams. Despite the measures introduced, coal mining was still a dangerous occupation and many accidents still occurred.

There are few areas in the borough of Rotherham that have not been blighted by the extraction of coal at one time or another. Most of Rotherham is situated above both shallow and deep seams of coal. Closely associated with coal mining were the coking plants and their unmistakable smell and deafening noise. Working conditions at the coking plants are often overlooked due to the number of deaths in the pits, but just as many deaths and injuries were reported in this industry as in the mines themselves, due to landslips of coal sidings, deaths in the furnaces, and accidents involving heavy plant machinery. Most of the time, this was due to the sheer noise made whilst producing coke; workers were seldom heard when in jeopardy.

Colliery waste tips, containing all the by-products that was not coal, were turned onto the land, creating vast slag heaps. The associated slurry ponds contained toxic chemicals that were extremely hazardous, resulting in the accidental deaths of people swimming and not knowing the dangers that lay beneath. Most of these areas are now in the process of being reclaimed and covered with housing, trading estates and light industry.

Maltby Colliery History

Maltby Colliery was sunk in 1908 by Maltby Main Colliery Company, a subsidiary of the Sheepbridge Iron and Coal Company. The colliery company employed Herbert Mollekin to build an estate of 1,000 houses for its employees. This was called the Model

Village and consisted of two concentric circles of roads; the miner's houses were on Scarborough Crescent to the rear, and the larger houses of Deacon Crescent, which were for the over men and deputies. It is the only pit in the area still being worked today.

Faces from the Flames

In an underground explosion in 1923, twenty-seven men were killed while trying to contain an underground fire. Rescue teams spent nineteen days below ground; sadly, only one body was ever recovered.

Since then men working at the pit face have often reported seeing miners with blistered faces, dressed in earlier attire with old Davy lamps, returning from where the said explosion had occurred all those years ago. However, due to the fear of ridicule, most accounts of this type are only ever shared amongst close workmates after a few drinks.

The Drunken Miner of Maltby

One warm September day in 2005, two local lads decided to take a dip in the pools at the bottom of the quarry, which was formally a slurry pit. On their way there, they were startled to meet a drunk, semi-naked miner, who they described as wearing a pair of shorts and pit boots, drinking from a bottle of cider. He stopped the lads and asked them where they were going. Knowing that they were trespassing, they said they were just hanging around,

to which the minor said, 'Come on lads, don't kid me on, tha's goin' fo' a swim in't quarry.' Trying to distance themselves from him, due to him being intoxicated, they quickened their pace, leaving the man shouting after them, 'Don't go swimming in the quarry, coz tha'll come a cropper like arr did.' Turning round, they saw the man enter an old sealed shaft entrance, and then vanish. At this disturbing sight and the ominous warning, the two lads decided not to go for a swim and instead hastily fled the scene.

Later that evening, one of the lads recounted the story to his grandfather, who used to work at the pit. He felt his blood run cold as the old man told him of a former pit colleague with a drinking problem, who was found dead. His body was not discovered until three weeks after he'd disappeared and was found face-down in the slurry pit, wearing just his shorts and boots. Investigations later revealed that he'd drowned while under the influence of alcohol, and recorded a verdict of accidental death.

Was this his warning to prevent the same auspicious death?

Silverwood Colliery

Silverwood Colliery was situated between the villages of Thrybergh and Ravenfield. Towards the end of the last century, when coal-mining was already a long-established industry in Yorkshire, the shallow seams in the western sector were used for the early miners to work by their primitive methods, but soon showed signs of becoming exhausted. So the private coal-owners of the time cast their eyes towards the much deeper reserves of rich coal there and the colliery grew into the Silverwood giant, as it was known. The shafts went down

An old winding wheel from lift shaft, which still stands at the entrance at Maltby. (Authors' collection)

The site of Silverwood now stands derelict.
(Authors' collection)

to the Barnsley seam, which was to become for many years the mainstay of Yorkshire mining.

Silverwood was placed among the million-ton-a-year collieries, making it one of the big-hitters of its time. Silverwood continued to provide employment for about 1,500 men, and make a valuable contribution to the prosperity of the local community. At over seventy years old, Silverwood had at least another half-century of good quality reserves to work. But like most pits in the 1080s, it was closed well before its time.

On Thursday, 3 February 1966, the paddy mail accident at Silverwood was to be a grim reminder of the dangers involved in working down the mines. The shift had started as normal and forty miners boarded the paddy train (nickname of the passenger train) for the journey to the pit face, a downhill run. Shortly after the train departed, a second train, known as the mail train, which carried the equipment, followed. The mail train suddenly went out of control, picking up speed, until it caught up with the train in front, smashing into the rear end.

The wreckage of the trains prevented easy access to the injured miners underground. For the families and friends, it meant a long and nerve-racking wait for news of who had survived and who had not, and at the end heartbreak for the families of the men who

had perished. Nine men died instantly in the disaster, one man died three days later in hospital, and thirty miners were injured. Some of the survivors were never to return underground again.

In the early 1980s, a young miner working at Silverwood colliery had an encounter with the paranormal. His story consequently became very well known, and aroused the interest of several researchers into the supernatural, as well as being reported in a number of national newspapers, including the *Morning Telegraph* and the *Sun*.

The miner was working underground with two colleagues, who were 300 yards ahead of him, when, without warning, a light appeared in the tunnel between himself and the others. As it seemed to be the headlamp of another miner, the collier waited for his approach. He noticed that the figure wore an old-style square pit helmet, a grubby waistcoat and dress shirt. As the stranger got closer, the young man bowed his head and the headlamp lit up the obscured miner's body. He stared in terror at what he saw. The stature of the man was normal in every respect, except for his face. The lamplight revealed a clearly defined neck and the shape of a head, but where the features should have been, such as eyes, nose and mouth, there was nothing ... only a blank space. The terrified miner dropped his equipment and ran screaming towards his colleagues. He was taken above ground suffering from shock. He swore that if he was not given a job on the pit surface, then he would resign, as he could never go underground again, such was his terror. Consequently, the young man took a considerable cut in wages to remain safely on the pit surface.

Could this be the shade of one of the men killed in the paddy mail accident?

Offices at the former pit site. (Authors' collection)

Kiveton Park Colliery History

The village of Kiveton Park, near Rotherham, was once rural and the main work was agricultural. In 1845 a railway was built through the district and almost twenty years later, coal mining became the mainstay at many locations along the line, including Kiveton. Kiveton Park Colliery was opened in 1864 and coal began being exported nationally by rail.

Kiveton Park was a relatively safe pit. However, accidents did occur. The worst accident at the colliery was in the nineteenth century, on 19 May 1889, when an underground explosion caused the untimely deaths of four miners.

The Engineer's Untold Story

In the 1980s, a pump fitter was called in to repair a breakage during one afternoon shift. Being a weekend shift, there were few men underground and the engineer travelled alone to the broken pump, about three miles from the bottom of the shaft. He had been gone for some time when he stunned colleagues by appearing, dazed and out of breath, back at the bottom of the shaft once more, having run the three miles from where the repair had been taking place. He was in deep shock, and could not utter a single word for over half an hour. Despite the requests of his workmates to find out what was wrong, he still would not speak about what he had witnessed, but something had horrified him so much that he refused to ever return to the seam in which he had been working.

In a subsequent conversation with the older colliers, who had been at Kiveton for many years, a local miner discovered that this area had once been the site of the fatal disaster. Could this explain the supernatural sighting? But the engineer still refuses to talk about the incident. To this day, nobody has any idea exactly what he saw.

Could he have witnessed the supernatural re-enacting of the explosion that happened in 1889?

Stubbin Pit

There were at least three pits at Stubbin, which was situated to the west of Rawmarsh. The land on which they stood belonged to Wentworth Estates and the pit was owned by Earl Fitzwilliam's Collieries Co. Ltd until nationalisation. The first sod of the new colliery development was cut by Viscount Milton, son of Earl Fitzwilliam, on 14 November 1913, and it took until 1915 to complete the sinking. One source has it that in 1920, Higher and Lower Stubbin Collieries closed. In 1933, Earl Fitzwilliam Collieries Co. registered and sank another pit called New Stubbin.

After 1948, the land was leased to British Coal. New Stubbin colliery ceased production on 6 June 1978, all the buildings were demolished and the railway ripped up. However, it remained as an underground store until the mid-1980s.

The lease expired more than a decade ago, and since then Wentworth Estates have been trying to find ways of making money from the site. Stubbin is a derelict site now, but you can still see the remains where the colliery once was.

The Vaporous Passenger

Today, if you walk along the old disused road towards the pit head, you can still see the remains of an old bus stop that once provided a service for the miners. Back then, public transport was heavily used and the services used to run in correspondence to shift patterns. After 1978, buses very rarely collected any passengers from this stop due to it falling into disuse.

Bus drivers working that route late at night would frequently see a man in a hard hat and overalls standing in the bus stop waiting to board. Thinking this was a passenger, they would stop and open the doors. The figure would approach to get on the bus, but at the point of boarding, he would evaporate into thin air.

Shocked drivers would return to Rawmarsh depot, refusing to work that route at night again. It is not known who the spectral figure is, or if there have been any further sightings of this vaporous passenger, due to the road and bus stop no longer being in use.

Dead Legs

Not too far away from the mine shaft is an old site, where the trains' coal buckets were stored during the time the mine was open. Today there are still the remains of old tracks and some rusted parts of disused carriages, along with the derelict walls of the ventilation shaft.

One summer's day in 2007, Richard was out walking his dogs down by the old vent

All that remains of the old bus shelter, where the figure was seen on many occasions. (Authors' collection)

shaft, which is overgrown by scrubland and bushes. He had just let the dogs off the lead and began to follow them at a leisurely pace, when a movement caught his eye underneath the scrubland. Thinking this was an animal, at first he didn't take much notice, but after taking a closer look he spotted some legs walking through the undergrowth parallel to him. Now, this wouldn't normally appear unusual, except the feet were underneath the bottom of the hedge of hawthorn trees, making it impossible for someone to walk that path due to the shear thickness of the thatch, which was already obscuring Richard's view of the figure's torso.

He described the legs as wearing work gear and mucky pit boots. At first he thought this was someone walking through a clearing that he wasn't aware of. Stopping in his tracks, he watched the legs disappear into the thick undergrowth. He raced along the footpath to investigate, so he could rationalise what he had just seen. But along the path there was no possible entrances. Eventually, he scrambled through the shrubbery to look for a clearing, but was astonished to see that not only was there no sign of the mystery person, but there was no access for anyone to walk either, just thick brambles.

Could these have been the legs of an old miner who worked the mines all those years ago? Or had Richard walked in a dead mans footsteps?

Wath Main Colliery (also known as Manvers)

Wath Main colliery and coking plant was one of South Yorkshire's biggest mines and wasn't shy to having a few ghost stories of its own. You would think most of these died when the pit was closed in the 1980s, but stories continue today from the men that worked there and visitors to the now redeveloped site.

The Menacing Miner of Wath Main

An outbreak of ghost sightings and supernatural encounters began to consume Wath Main to such an extent, that the hardened miners of South Yorkshire refused to work in groups of less than five. Fear of the 'Menacing Miner' became rife and sparked a media frenzy, with stories consequently appearing in such newspapers as the *Star*, the *Telegraph*, and the *South Yorkshire Times*.

The first terrifying encounter occurred when a group of miners shoring up the ceiling supports before the main shift started, saw a pit lamp approach. The gang downed tools and waited for the man to identify himself; this was protocol for safety reasons. The light continued towards them until it was within twenty yards; they could hear his footsteps approaching but couldn't see him, just the lamp. As the miner began to get close enough to be identified, the light vanished.

Concerned at the disappearance of the light, thinking their mate had fallen over and broken his lamp or possibly injured himself, the gang ran down the tunnel to see what had happened to him. They were unnerved when they discovered that there was no one there, and even more worried when they found that there was nowhere for him to go; the only way out would have been past them.

Dismissing what they'd seen, they went back up the shaft and resumed checking the props and sprags, working towards where they had seen the light. As they reached the

All that's left of the once mighty Manvers Coking Plant. (Authors' collection)

point where the phantom had vanished, they were horrified to discover that the roof supports had been sabotaged.

Multiple ominous encounters of this nature followed, and on all occasions equipment was found to have been tampered with. Panic spread like wildfire throughout Wath colliery, causing unrest in the workforce.

Research reveals that a miner had in fact died tragically at this precise part of the works where the 'Menacing Miner' had appeared; this fuelled the miner's fear into a frenzy, alerting media attention. The eerie encounters undoubtedly converted disbelievers into believing that a supernatural presence did indeed exist. Others, who claimed to have seen nothing, chose not to believe, yet they still refused to work there alone!

The Black Widow of Wath

On 9 September 2010, a man was camping along with his son and a friend in the grounds of Cusworth Hall in Barnsley. Deciding to move on to pastures new, they headed towards the old Manvers Pit site in Wath.

Arriving at dusk, they headed towards the park entrance at the point where Dearne Road and Station Road meet, which is locally known as a notorious accident blackspot. Upon approach, they could see the figure of a woman on the opposite side of the road, who seemed to be floating along the path. Not believing their own eyes, they maintained a distance between themselves and the figure, but continued as they were heading that way anyway. They had the strange feeling that she was enticing them to follow.

She then flew across the road into the entrance of the park, where they were going to set up camp. They described her as being dressed in a black hooded cloak and moving in a strobe-like fashion. The trio followed the winding paths in to the park, but lost sight of her and decided to set up camp in a small clearing near the river. All of a sudden they felt a noticeable drop in temperature, and, looking up, they were horrified to discover that the woman was standing around 30 yards away, staring straight at them from the faceless opening of her cloak.

The group were scared to death by the encounter and the father started to panic. Not wanting to alarm the children, he ushered them out of the park and frantically telephoned his friend to come and collect them immediately. He said that waiting at the gates for his lift seemed to take an eternity, and the feeling of dread was insurmountable.

The father later described that they felt an evil presence closing in on them, as if they were being followed and watched. Even as he recounted this to us he had an uneasy feeling and advised us that if anyone was going to investigate this, then they should go in a group of four or more, and never to venture there alone.

We have both been to investigate this report on numerous occasions, but have yet to track down the Black Widow of Wath …

Dinnington Colliery

Pit deputies held a responsible position as they were accountable for the safety of the men underground. Their duties included overseeing the setting of pit props to support the roof and ensuring there was no subsidence, as well as checking that the mine was well ventilated. They would go down to check the coal seams before the shift started, and it was common practice for them to do this alone.

Decades ago, one such man had gone to look at a particular seam and sat down to have his break before resuming his duties. Whilst

pouring himself a cup of tea from his flask, he noticed a light approaching him in the distance, which got brighter as it came towards him, until a miner appeared with his head-lamp on. The deputy did not recognize him but greeted him anyway with a cheery 'ey up.' The miner replied 'all right cock,' then passed him and carried on his way further down the tunnel, towards a disused seem. The deputy was a little puzzled why the miner should be going towards a district that had closed several years earlier. As he watched, the miner's head-lamp finally disappeared into the dark shaft.

At the end of the shift, the deputy came up and asked his mate on the surface, 'Who's the new deputy workin' on't told pit face, are they oppening it back up?' In reply, his mate told him, 'I don't no what tha's on about – tha was down there on thee own, nobody's been up or down whilst I've been here. I reckon tha's just seen the ghost that haunts the old seem.' The deputy never saw the ghostly stranger again.

Many heard of this phantom and sightings were reported on numerous occasions. Safety standards were not as stringent as they are in modern mining, and accidents were commonplace. Who is to say that one of these departed miners does not still work the empty pit today?

The Miner of the Lamp

Another ghost said to haunt Dinnington colliery was a man who appeared above ground as opposed to below. At night, the colliery buildings were lit by floor-mounted floodlights for the men on late shifts. On several occasions, the large outline of a man was to be seen looming against one of the building walls, as though someone was blocking the light from the lamp itself. This was so common that miners used to race towards the light source to try and catch whoever it was, but there was never anyone there.

All that's left of Dinningtton Colliery. (Authors' collection)